Praise for *Mentor for Life*

The invitation that Jesus extended to the first who followed him is one that he continues to extend to us. It is an invitation to "intentional discipleship," characterized by developing a life of being with him, being shaped and empowered by him, and being sent on mission for him. Natasha Robinson carefully sets forth a very powerful and practical way that this is done . . . it is a welcome gift for the whole Body of Christ.

—Bishop (Dr.) Claude Alexander Jr., Senior
Pastor, The Park Church, Charlotte, NC

Natasha has not only written a very fine book about mentoring, she actually serves as a mentor for us, her readers. This volume is an expert guide, a model, a voice to give us the courage to respond to Jesus' call to make disciples. May each of us follow her lead, and in response, lead others in fruitful discipleship.

—Tracy Balzer, Director of Christian Formation,
John Brown University; author, *Permission to Ponder:
Contemplative Wisdom for the Spiritually Distracted*

Bold and wise, *Mentor for Life* is an intentional discipleship guide for the women who officially or unofficially lead others. With refreshing boldness, this book trains and equips leaders for a great purpose.

—Sarah Bessey, author, *Out of Sorts: Making Peace
with an Evolving Faith* and *Jesus Feminist*

"Spiritual growth is something we do by ourselves and is between us and God." That's a very American thought, but it has nothing to do with biblical Christianity. Natasha Sistrunk Robinson explains clearly not only why Christians need to mentor and be mentored but how to best go about it. The information in *Mentor for Life* will revolutionize your spiritual life.

—Shane Blackshear, host of podcast *Seminary
Dropout*, ShaneBlackshear.com

With passion and clarity, Natasha Sistrunk Robinson has presented a case for mentorship that conveys both the urgency of the mission and a vision for execution. *Mentor for Life* is written with the real world in mind and provides a framework that is relevant to real people. If you want to engender a stronger faith in yourself and others, Robinson has offered up a valuable resource.

—Richard Clark, Managing Editor, *Leadership Journal*, Christianity Today

Mentor for Life is a must-read for anyone who is serious about developing and deepening those they mentor. Robinson doesn't just show us "the city on the hill" but gives a roadmap on how to get there. If you are serious about mentoring, then start here.

—Rodney L. Cooper, PhD, the Kenneth and Jean Hansen Professor of Discipleship and Leadership, Gordon-Conwell Theological Seminary

With clear focus on Jesus' priorities, Natasha leads us to love God, to love others, and to make disciples. She demonstrates that this kind of growth and maturity in the child of God happens best in a mentoring relationship. Foundational reasoning and practical teaching and examples make this a fabulous tool for any church or ministry desiring to build multiplying disciples.

—Judy Douglass, Global Leadership and Director, Women's Resources, Cru (formerly Campus Crusade for Christ)

There is no higher calling upon an individual believer, or more accurate measure of his or her spiritual maturity, than the practice of reproducing Christlike faith in the life of another. In *Mentor for Life*, Natasha thinks deeply, writes passionately, and challenges practically with the goal of helping you pursue and fulfill the Great Commission one life at a time.

—Dr. Mark DeYmaz, Directional Leader, Mosaic Church of Central AR; author, *MIX: Transitioning Your Church to Living Color*

Mentor for Life is a wonderful resource for women. Natasha's passion for mentorship and discipleship is both challenging and contagious. This is a great book that will encourage, challenge, and equip women to think more theologically about mentorship and discipleship and will move them into action.

—Lesley Hildreth, Assistant Director of Women's Life,
Southeastern Baptist Theological Seminary

Natasha has laid out a vision for mentoring that incorporates women of all generations, life circumstances, and cultures. The emphasis on mentoring within a group is incredibly helpful, and it invites mutual, intentional relationships where everyone leaves knowing God, themselves, and one another better. The questions included throughout the book make this an excellent tool to use in a mentoring small group, especially for those looking to start mentoring groups in their church.

Amy Jackson, Managing Editor, *SmallGroups.com*, Christianity Today

Natasha Sistrunk Robinson is a truth-teller, and the truth is we need truth-tellers. In her book, *Mentor for Life: Finding Purpose through Intentional Discipleship*, you will encounter a fundamental truth: we all need mentors as we make our way through this messy complicated world. Read this book and be encouraged.

—Dr. Frank A. James III, President, Biblical Theological Seminary

To know my friend Natasha is to know a woman whose heart is compelled by the church, deep rooted community, relationships that matter, and a palpable love of Jesus. So it's no wonder that she has written *Mentor for Life* . . . I am grateful for this book and look forward to sharing it with my daughters when they grow up.

—Eddie Kaufholz, writer; cohost, *RELEVANT*
podcast; speaker, International Justice Mission

In a culture that prides itself on individual strength, growth, and determination, Natasha Robinson invites the reader to imagine the kingdom vision of the Bible—communal strength. . . . Not only does Robinson make a strong biblical and theological case for mentoring and discipleship, she also inspires the reader to implement the models laid out in the book. I personally am excited to see the fruits of this lovely and insightful book.

—Tara Beth Leach, Director of Women's
Ministry, Christ Church of Oak Brook

Mentor for Life is a much-needed reminder of the call to discipleship, particularly a discipleship that is inclusive of those who have historically been marginalized within the evangelical church. Robinson's words are at once inspiring and convicting to the gathering of believers we call the church . . . Thank you Natasha, for this reminder of what it means to be the church.

—Rev. Dr. Michelle R. Lloyd-Paige, Executive Associate to the President for Diversity and Inclusion, Calvin College

I believe in the power of circles of women, and Natasha Sistrunk Robinson has created a model of mentoring by which we can grow in intimacy with God as we journey with each other. There is so much hope, growth, and freedom possible when we gather in these ways, intentionally, authentically, and always with Jesus at the center.

—Idelette McVicker, founder, *SheLovesmagazine.com*

Thick with biblical and practical wisdom, *Mentor for Life* will prove to be a helpful resource for those wanting to begin or improve the discipleship initiatives of their local church. But one danger will always remain: Will we, as Robinson warns, crowd our lives with lesser things?

—Jen Pollock Michel, author, *Teach Us to Want*

In putting mentoring as an intentional means of discipleship back on the radar, my friend Natasha Robinson has offered pastors and lay leaders alike a tremendous gift, one that I think could help to spark a much-needed revolution in the formation of Christian disciples and leaders for God's mission.

—JR Rozko, Codirector, Missio Alliance

Too often writers piecemeal their approach to outreach and discipleship. Not Natasha Sistrunk Robinson. Among the many powerful chapters in this book, "Connecting Evangelism and Discipleship" is a standout. She has done the church a great service by carefully and clearly explaining how growth in Christ, service to the needy, and personal mentoring are essential elements in every person's spiritual journey.

—Bob Whitesel, DMin, award-winning author of twelve books; founding professor of Wesley Seminary at Indiana Wesleyan University

Mentor
for Life

Mentor for Life

Finding Purpose through Intentional Discipleship

Natasha Sistrunk Robinson

ZONDERVAN

Mentor for Life
Copyright © 2016 by Natasha Sistrunk Robinson

This title is also available as a Zondervan ebook.
Visit www.zondervan.com/ebooks.

Requests for information should be addressed to:
Zondervan, 3900 *Sparks Dr. SE, Grand Rapids, Michigan 49546*

Library of Congress Cataloging-in-Publication Data

Names: Robinson, Natasha Sistrunk, 1979-
Title: Mentor for life: finding purpose through intentional discipleship / Natasha
    Sistrunk Robinson.
Description: Grand Rapids: Zondervan, 2016. | Includes bibliographical references.
Identifiers: LCCN 2015036838 | ISBN 9780310522355 (softcover)
Subjects: LCSH: Mentoring—Religious aspects—Christianity. | Discipling
    (Christianity) | Church work with women. | Christian women—Religious life.
Classification: LCC BV4408.5 .R63 2016 | DDC 253/.7—dc23 LC record available at
    http://lccn.loc.gov/2015036838

Published in association with the literary agency of Credo Communications, LLC,
Grand Rapids, MI 49525; www.credocommunications.net.

Art direction: Holly Sharp Creative
Interior design: Kait Lamphere

Printed in the United States of America

16 17 18 19 20 21 22 23 24 25 26 /DHV/ 15 14 13 12 11 10 9 8 7 6 5 4 3 2 1

For Deronta, my homey, lover, friend.

For Ashley, from creation, through Scripture, until now, may you see God's hand at work in your legacy before you were even born.

In Memoriam
Sallie F. Johnson (December 7, 1946–December 9, 1999)
My Mentor. My Mom.

Contents

Foreword

In so many ways, I am who I am today because of the mentors God has placed in my life. When I became a Christian in high school, living in inner-city Minneapolis, a youth pastor named Art Erickson mentored me and two other young men who had recently come to know Christ. In that small group, I learned much about the Scriptures and what it meant to be a follower of Christ, and I began to discover my leadership abilities.

During my senior year in college, I began to wrestle with a call to ministry. I went to my girlfriend (who is now my wife) and asked to talk to her grandfather, Dr. Edward Berry Sr., who was serving as a pastor. He offered words of wisdom and advice to me, and several months later, I began meeting with him and a young man named Dennis Carter. That two-year mentoring relationship eventually led to me becoming a licensed and ordained minister. Over those two years, Dennis and I learned what it meant to be a minister of the gospel through the tough love, care, wisdom, and intentionality of this seasoned pastor, a man who was willing to teach as long as we were willing to receive.

My life continues to be impacted by male and female mentors. Dr. Brenda Salter-McNeil has been like a big sister, helping me discover my call to speak and write on racial reconciliation and biblical justice. Pastor Gerald Joiner and Dr. J. Alfred Smith, Sr. have provided me with insights on how to serve as a healthy and fruitful pastor for the long haul. Dr. Robert Owens and Reverend Gary Walter have mentored me in executive and apostolic leadership. I confess that I've been spoiled with excellent mentors!

I know I am a more faithful and fruitful disciple, servant, and leader because these people have poured their words and wisdom into my life. As they have been faithful to the biblical mandate to make disciples, pouring their lives into mine, I have developed clarity in my call and focus for my life mission.

As grateful as I am for the mentoring I have received over the years, my heart breaks when I think of the countless people in the local church—across the United States and beyond—who have not had someone to mentor them. They have not personally experienced the power of the Great Commission. There are far too many who attend church but whose lives still lack the spiritual empowerment an intentional mentoring community can provide. There are people who come to Christ and find a church home, but they never get started on the revolutionary journey of becoming a mature follower of Christ. They never receive the missional charge that accompanies their kingdom citizenship.

I believe this is a major reason why the church in the United States lacks transforming power. The church faces a crisis of declining attendance and a growing dissatisfaction with institutionalized Christianity. There are large metropolitan areas populated by unchurched millennials who attend churches where there is too much emphasis on experiential worship and a watered down approach to discipleship. Even as we see more and more mega-churches, and as church planting becomes the latest fad, without a radical prioritizing of discipleship, our fruitfulness in advancing the kingdom of God will be limited. Evangelism is liberating and leads to eternal life, but discipleship is what we need to raise up an army of kingdom laborers, ambassadors of reconciliation, and agents of God's glory.

In *Mentor for Life*, Natasha Robinson moves discipleship "out-of-the-box," beyond an individualized approach, emphasizing that while mentoring bears fruit in one-to-one, life-on-life experiences, it truly flourishes in a more communal, small group setting. A small group approach to mentoring is not a new discovery, but it is an important way of empowering disciples and helping them discover their life missions.

We live in an increasingly multiethnic, multicultural mission field. And part of this new reality is the widening divide between the haves and the have-nots. There is a great need to raise up disciples who can advance the kingdom of God across cultures and empower the poor and marginalized in their midsts. Ms. Robinson assists us in this missional endeavor.

Finally, I am especially thankful that this book focuses on the connection between discipleship and the empowerment of women. It's easy to read through the Gospels and jump over the powerful encounters between Christ and women. We still struggle within the body of Christ to recognize the kingdom advancing the potential of our sisters, valuing what they can contribute to the Church. As someone who has been personally impacted by the preaching, teaching, and leadership of women—and as the father of two teenage daughters—I see the importance of mentoring initiatives that will bring forth the next generation of female pastors, evangelists, and apostolic servants. Women have played such a significant role in church planting, missions, and the development of the church as a refuge that it would be a shame if we didn't create mentoring space for girls and women to experience the life-giving empowerment of the Spirit. My heart pounds with joy when I think about how this book will help to fuel such a movement.

I realize this is not the first book written on discipleship and mentoring. But it is a necessary one. The best way to help others see the need for mentoring is to share how mentoring has made a difference in your own life, and Ms. Robinson does that. She shares a practical theology filled with biblical insights, and she points us toward ministry models that work in the local church.

Reverend Efrem Smith
President and CEO of World Impact and author
of *Jump: Into a Life of Further and Higher*

The Mentoring Vision

Every one of us wants to know our purpose in this world. Maybe that desire begins with asking questions about a familiar name or family history. As we grow older, we may start thinking about our legacy or the lessons we want to pass on to our children and others whom we have the privilege of influencing. Sometimes finding that purpose causes us to jump around a bit, make mistakes, or go out to explore the world. Understanding purpose can be a slow process that is shepherded by the humble presence and support of a mentor.

As I write and minister, it becomes more evident to me that Christian women want to participate in the work of God in their churches, and they want authentic mentoring that will challenge their growth in Christ and their relationships with others. I rejoice with the women who have rewarding mentoring relationships, and my heart breaks for those who are still searching but have no one to mentor them.

I am a beneficiary of mentoring. Through the support of my parents and the loving training of countless mentors, I have been allowed to realize my leadership potential. Even as a child, I learned to communicate honestly, articulate clearly, and to humbly say "thank you" for opportunities and opened doors; to travel; to negotiate; to plan; to build teams, manage projects, and implement change. As a young visionary, I was able to lead. Those leadership experiences were transformative and eventually led to me attending the United States Naval Academy. There I began military training and a career that filled eleven years of my adult life. Each of our lives is shaped by brief moments captured in time; therefore, you will notice that my military and leadership training have infused the pages of this book.

I am keenly aware that the military analogies may make some readers uncomfortable. When sharing these stories, I am not encouraging or endorsing all military action; rather, I am seeking to connect practical life experiences to the military themes already present in the Bible. The apostle Paul wrote the majority of the New Testament to an audience familiar with the militarization of its culture, and he used language to identify with them and explain the hope of the gospel. As disciples of Christ, we have a deeper understanding of biblical messages when we have a better knowledge of military culture. This book will allow you to see Scripture in a different light as my personal stories and military metaphors communicate key biblical principles that relate to mentoring for God's kingdom purposes.

I want you to catch this vision! Imagine: what would happen if *every* Christian committed to making discipleship a priority in his or her life and local church? What would happen if Christians embraced mentoring as a means of holistic discipleship, through which we captivate the minds of individuals so they learn how to think theologically and live out the truth of the whole gospel we claim to believe? What would happen if all believers understood and embraced their identity in Christ, and truly lived as transformed people under the power of the Holy Spirit? What would happen if we all mentored for life?

About This Book

This book is divided into two parts. Part I answers the question, "Why do we need mentoring in the church?" It clearly defines mentoring as intentional discipleship and presents the big picture of mentoring for God's kingdom. Collectively, the chapters in Part I also answer the "So what?" question. God is at work in the world through the power of the Holy Spirit. Mentoring and making disciples is the catalyst for his work going forward. Our love for God and others, the commission and resurrective power of Christ, along with our concerns for the church and the needs of the world are what compels us and sustains us in this work.

Chapter 1 is your invitation to join God's mission and see the benefits of mentoring in the body of Christ. Chapter 2 briefly explores the traditional evangelical movement in America and how mentoring bridges the separation between the church's traditional approach to evangelism and Jesus' command to make disciples. Chapter 3 acknowledges the challenges we face in our culture, the temptations we wrestle with in the church, and presents mentoring as a tool God uses to change our hearts, the church, culture, and community. Chapter 4 puts mentoring within the context of God's kingdom. Mentoring as intentional discipleship helps us understand what we are spiritually up against as children of God and how God purposes for us to create a culture that glorifies him.

Part II presents the foundational commitments of mentoring. These include:

- Presence: Being present with God and present in community with other disciples is essential for our spiritual transformation.
- Discipline: Cultivating spiritual disciples helps us recognize our spiritual poverty and desperate need for God.
- Mission: Understanding God's kingdom mission gives us an urgency and intentionality to run our own spiritual race

and to invite others to win on the journey of following Christ.

- Community: Committing to safe and trusting mentoring relationships provides encouragement, accountability, and support.
- Relationships: Mentoring requires that we embrace people as God does and welcome diverse relationships that reflect true unity in the body of Christ.
- Love: Mentoring is a continuous sacrificial and selfless act of love that shapes our character, clarifies our spiritual gifts, and affirms our purpose and calling.

Understanding and remembering these commitments are necessary for those embarking on the journey of mentoring. These commitments will inform the questions you ask and the decisions you make moving forward. A "This Is How We Do It" section is included at the end of each commitment summary to help you get started and to provide a snapshot of what implementing the mentoring commitment can look like in a church ministry.

My hope is that you will be spiritually formed by going through this book with other leaders or in a mentoring community. I have included questions at the end of each chapter to allow for personal reflection and application. Part II also includes personal mentoring exercises to reinforce each mentoring commitment.

Who Is This Book For?

This book is written from the perspective of mentoring within the context of a small group community (ideally four to six people) instead of one-on-one mentoring relationships. It is primarily for current and aspiring leaders who desire to prioritize discipleship in their local congregations or those who want to provide a more substantive teaching and training ministry. The principles shared are applicable for those who have a burning passion to serve God and his people. On the other hand, not everyone has the skills or the desire to effectively lead a church ministry. You, too, can advance God's kingdom by investing in the lives of others and applying these mentoring principles within a small mentoring group right in your living room or dorm room.

Mentor for Life challenges and equips you to train and raise the standard of expectations for "laypeople" in your congregation. Those who are young in their faith, beginners, or mentees may wonder, "What's in this book for me?" There are countless legitimate reasons why now may not be the best time for you to lead a mentoring group. As you read, the question of consideration maybe not be, "God, are you desiring that I start or lead a mentoring ministry?" Your questions may be much simpler, like "God, how might you use this book to encourage and teach me to follow you wholeheartedly?" Or "How might I embrace the biblical principles of this book to teach and train my children to follow you?" The good news is that whether you are leading, following, or learning, God has provided relationships to help you live with Christ in view, with the power of the Holy Spirit inside you, and with great hope and anticipation for your future.

While reading, will you purpose to (1) evaluate your spiritual condition, (2) consider your commitment to God's kingdom work, and (3) prioritize making disciples? It is my hope and prayer that you will be encouraged in those intentions, and that this mentoring manifesto will inspire you to know and love God, know who you are in Christ, and love your neighbor as yourself.

Part One

The Mentoring Call to Action

Purpose and Priorities

Mentoring and making disciples in the midst of our crazy, fallen world and hectic lives can be challenging. When life is difficult, some people dig in their heels and work harder, while others throw up their hands and quit. Before we look at specific mentoring principles and practices, I'd like to clarify the purpose and priorities of mentoring.

I invite you to join the mentoring mission, and in that vein, I want to first lay a theological foundation for you. I hope this foundation will sustain you when you lack confidence, when the road gets difficult, or when you are heartbroken and want to give up. Be encouraged that you are not alone on this journey and that there is great joy in living your life for God's purposes. I'd like to suggest that you meditate on the following focus areas as you read through Part I of this book: Christ, conviction, courage, and confidence.

Christ

Christ's finished work on the cross allows us to live as free and flourishing people. Christ sent the Holy Spirit to empower us to live as transformed servants, surrendered to God. When we mentor from the perspective of intentional discipleship, we are embracing God's kingdom work. God is the author of the entire story of Scripture, and he has given each of us a script or role to play in his grand narrative. God wants us to get involved and join in his work. In what is sometimes referred to as his High Priestly Prayer, Jesus said, "I have brought you [the Father] glory on earth by finishing the work you gave me to do" (John 17:4). Like Christ, we each have a choice to glorify God with our lives and through our work. We glorify God by agreeing with his desire to change the hearts and minds of people, and by mentoring them to align their lives and will to his good vision for the world. Through mentoring, we have the honor and privilege of joining God in his work of transformation.

Conviction

We need to understand the pressing issues of the church and culture so we have a relevant, urgent, and practical application for our learning. We also need a biblical framework and theological conviction that informs why we should pursue mentoring in the first place. Together we will ponder, "What does the Bible actually say about making disciples?" and "How does the church practice this conviction?" Like the writers of the New Testament, we will also consider if any good lessons can be learned from the philosophers of old or from our current culture. Together, we will allow the Scriptures to reveal our blind spots. Then, we will move forward with confidence and courage as we prepare our hearts for mentoring.

Courage

Will we make disciples? This is a courageous question. The Old Testament admonishes us to seek wisdom, knowledge, and understanding. A wise person is discerning. Sometimes we know what is right and we simply lack the courage to do it. In the Old Testament, Solomon and Joshua both knew what right actions to take, although courage historically separates the moral falling away of Solomon and the mighty victories of Joshua. James, a disciple of Jesus, gives us a stern warning: "If anyone, then, knows the good they ought to do and doesn't do it, it is sin for them" (4:17). Sometimes our sin is not as blatant as Solomon's transgressions. We don't boldly declare to God, "I will not make disciples." We simply crowd our lives with a lot of *good* things that become idols and leave no space for the very things God says must be a priority for *all* Christians—mainly, loving him, loving our neighbors, and making disciples of Jesus Christ. It is not enough for us to know what the right things are; we need courage to do them. Until this point, fear might have kept you from intentionally making disciples. I understand. Sometimes our godly work assignments can be intimidating, but Dr. Halee Gray Scott reminds us that, "courage is not the absence of fear but the willingness to move forward despite fear."[1] Indeed, courage calls us to commit to mentoring others in spite of our fears.

Confidence

It is humbling to know God has written us into his story and wants to use us for his kingdom purposes. It is also comforting to understand that in spite of our best efforts, "success" in mentoring does not depend on us. It is God alone who changes hearts, transforms lives, and brings us all into alignment with his vision for the world. He does this through the work of the Holy Spirit. By committing to mentoring, we avail ourselves to the transformation process. We can have great joy in living our lives for God's purposes. This, my friends, is the best way to live!

When our priorities are in order, our lives have clearer focus, and fulfillment in our lives on this earth can be a by-product of our obedience. A common saying goes, "Be the kind of woman who, when your feet hit the floor in the morning, the Devil says, 'Oh no, She's up.'" I don't wake up wondering whether my day is going to count or if my life matters, because my confidence lies in the person and finished work of Christ. My identity rests in him, and for that reason, I have accepted the work he has assigned to me. You, too, can have this same confidence in living your life on mission for Christ, and you can start by mentoring for Christ's kingdom purposes.

One

Join the Mission

The transformational leader motivates us to do more than we
expected to do, by raising our awareness of different values,
by getting us to transcend our self-interests for the cause and
by expanding our portfolio of needs and wants.
Leighton Ford[1]

"Let's talk about your passion for mentoring. Do you think it's because you lost your mother?"

My mentor asked this question during one of our times together.

I could see why she would think that. It would be easy to conclude that a young girl who had lost her mother during college would naturally cling to older women to fill her "mommy void." But that just wasn't the case. My mom died when I was a twenty-year-old sophomore at the U.S. Naval Academy. She had loved me deeply. There was nothing lacking in our relationship. She was one of several people who mentored me in my formative years, and when I left home for college, I gained more mentors still.

By the time I graduated from college, mentoring was in my DNA; it had become a burning passion. Truthfully, I owe that passion and my gratitude to all the mentors who have invested in me faithfully over the years. But mentoring has brought more than a driving purpose to my life. It also has ushered in inexpressible joy as I participate in the kingdom of God on this earth. And no wonder: this mission is exactly what you and I are made for. Allow me to explain.

College is where I learned that mentoring at its best is a mutual relationship cultivated for a specific purpose or mission. Mentoring relationships are intentional, and they are built on the trust and understanding that exists between those who are mentoring and those who are being mentored. So even in the sharing of this book, I believe you and I are mutually growing in our ability to mentor and be mentored. By presenting the kingdom vision and mission of mentoring, I am inviting you to participate in God's mission and purpose to flourish in our lives, in our communities, in our culture, and in the world in which we live.

I don't know how you feel about invitations, but as I grow in wisdom, I am more cautious about the invitations I accept. Sometimes I'm invited to an event I don't think will be fun, so I don't go. At other times, I am invited to parties where I can kick off my shoes, shake out my hair, and let loose. I'm glad to accept those invitations because many years ago I learned to work hard and play hard. I learned to prioritize and invest in the important things of life, and I am learning to enjoy the rewards and benefits of those investments. When you have covered your bases and handled your business, it's okay to occasionally go to a party!

At some point during my faith journey, somebody described heaven to me as one big party. I don't think that's a complete understanding of what we have to look forward to in heaven, but I do believe we will experience unimaginable joy for all eternity when we enter the presence of God. By answering the call to discipleship, we have an opportunity to partake in a part of the kingdom of heaven now—because we can experience great joy in living our lives with God's kingdom mission in view.

We cannot continually hold on to our own lives and our own ways of doing things, yet embrace the purpose and priorities of God at the same time. They are in conflict with each other. I don't know exactly what that means for you personally, but Dietrich Bonhoeffer calls us to ponder:

If we answer the call to discipleship, where will it lead us? What decisions and partings will it demand? To answer these questions we shall have to go to him, for only he knows the answer. Only Jesus Christ, who bids us follow him, knows the journey's end. But we do know that it will be a road of boundless mercy. Discipleship means joy.[2]

With joy, I pray that our dreams for the redemption of the church, our communities, and our culture are not deferred. I pray that the desire for mentoring does not simply come across as a brilliant idea. Mentoring is indeed a great idea, but some great ideas are never realized, in part due to our lack of courage. May it not be so with mentoring. May it not be so with you.

I pray that the reality of your commitment to mentoring is better than what you can imagine right now as you read this book. God in his mighty power can make that happen! I pray that you will find your unique means of contribution, the ways you alone were created to glorify God in this great world. I pray that as we look forward with great anticipation to the return of Christ, you embrace the call to mentor and make disciples. I pray that we will accept the challenge to personally prioritize both the "Great Commandment" to love and the "Great Commission" to make disciples. I pray that you will gain a new understanding of mentoring to build on for the rest of your life.

Reevaluating the History of Mentoring and Leadership

I sat across the table from the discipleship pastor of my church during the bustling lunch hour at the local Panera Bread. Over clanging saucers, business conversations, and buzzing cell phones, he spoke words I was thrilled to hear: "Natasha, I want to talk to you about offering training so we can launch a men's and women's mentoring ministry at our church. I know we need to be more intentional about discipling people." I was elated that he so clearly understood the church's need.

"I'm glad to help," I said. "How can I be of service?"

We shared our hearts for discipleship and the people of God. Then he asked me, "Why do you call it mentoring? Why not just call it discipleship?"

So I explained:

"Part of our responsibilities as leaders is to understand where people are before we consider where we want to motivate them to go. I'm not convinced that the average Sunday worshipper or the new believer really understands what discipleship is. I would love to survey the church to see how laypeople actually define discipleship, and of equal importance, I would love to challenge every Christian as to whether they are actually making disciples in their own areas of influence. As leaders, we would like to conclude that discipleship is common language, common understanding, and common practice in the church, but often it is not. Since this is not language all Christians understand and communicate, I use the word *mentoring*, which is more familiar, to essentially get people on track toward understanding the mission of discipleship."

Merriam-Webster's dictionary defines a mentor as a "trusted counselor or guide; a tutor, coach."[3] In Homer's classic, *The Odyssey*, the warrior Odysseus leaves his son, Telemachus, in the hands of a man named Mentor, who takes responsibility for instructing and advising the young man.[4] Some philosophers think this is where the word "mentor" originates; however, the concept of mentoring does not find its roots in Greek mythology, nor is it limited to coaching or advising someone. The truth is, the roots of mentoring are found in the Bible, and when we take a biblical approach to mentoring, we discover that it is far more than simply pointing someone in the right direction.

The Old Testament provides several mentoring relationships

to consider: Elijah and Elisha, Eli and Samuel, Moses and Joshua, and Naomi and Ruth. The New Testament Gospels also present a picture of Jesus as mentor. Jesus prayerfully handpicked twelve disciples and called them to give up everything and follow him. He taught and trained them so they, in turn, would teach and train others to follow him as well. Through intimate communion with his heavenly Father, he modeled a life of *being* in God's presence and then humbly *doing* everything his Father commanded. He taught his disciples what it means to be a true leader—to be a servant to others. He grew their wisdom and knowledge, journeyed with them through life's messes and suffering, and called them his friends. Jesus was the image they were to reflect to the rest of the world. He was the perfect mentor.

The Bible teaches us that true mentoring extends beyond the definition we find in the dictionary or the understanding we can gain from Greek mythology. Yes, skills like counseling, coaching, and guiding are important aspects of mentoring, but there is much more to it than that. Advice comes cheap these days, and people don't need one more person telling them what to do. They need people of wisdom who can speak God's truths, while equipping and encouraging them to live their lives on purpose for him. When we consider mentoring from a Christian perspective, the responsibilities are greater because the impact is eternal.

Regi Campbell, author of *Mentor Like Jesus*, writes, "Mentoring is not about coming *to know* something; that would be education. Mentoring isn't about learning *to do* something; that would be training. Mentoring is about showing someone how *to be something*. It's about *becoming* a learner and follower of Jesus Christ."[5]

After much thought and practice, I've come to this definition of mentoring:

> *Mentoring is a trusted partnership where people share wisdom that fosters spiritual growth and leads to transformation as mentors and mentees[6] grow in their love of Christ, knowledge of self, and love of others.*

If we adopt the view that mentoring fosters spiritual growth that compels us to follow Jesus Christ, and that it leads us to surrender to the change needed for spiritual maturity, then we are led to the following conclusions about the relationship between mentoring and discipleship:

1. God's kingdom purposes for mentorship and discipleship are one and the same. The words can be used synonymously when *any* Christian assumes the responsibility of influence in the life of another.
2. As Christians, when we mentor others, our primary purpose is to make disciples of Christ and to show them how they can make disciples of Christ.

To put it simply: **mentoring is *intentional discipleship*.**

Mentoring Fundamentals

"I'm going back to school," said Mandy. She was clearly both excited and a little fearful. A hospice nurse in her second year of mentoring, Mandy struggled to adjust to life as a new student, working mom, and wife.

Sometime during her first semester, I checked in to provide words of encouragement and some tough love regarding Mandy's need for self-discipline and perseverance. Within a few months, she was thriving. She later called to say, "Thank you so much for giving us challenging resources to read and having us write our reflections and articulate our thoughts. I have not read for the purpose of comprehension since high school, and I would not be prepared for college had it not been for the mentoring ministry. Because of mentoring, my papers are easy and I don't fear sharing with others during class presentations." Ah, the joy of mentoring!

This simple revelation and blessing in Mandy's life can be a source of encouragement for each of us, regardless of our life stage.

Although Mandy initially pursued the mentoring ministry with caution, she commited to her mentoring small group. Since her mentoring group only gathered once per month, showing up regularly was not a huge time commitment. As a full-time working wife, mom, and student, she judged rightly that she was not in the position to lead a mentoring group. Although she understood it was not her time to lead, she quickly embraced that it is always a time to learn about God, his kingdom, and his purposes.

Mentoring is about leading and learning, following and listening. Preparation is always for a future day, so when we are asked to lead, we are ready. As a leader committed to mentoring as intentional discipleship, I am keenly aware of the responsibility to continually challenge and move people along on their faith journeys regardless of life stage. After writing about the fundmentals and assurance of the Christian faith, the writer of Hebrews continues:

> We have much to say about this, but it is hard to make it clear to you because you no longer try to understand. In fact, though by this time you ought to be teachers, you need someone to teach you the elementary truths of God's word all over again. You need milk, not solid food! Anyone who lives on milk, being still an infant, is not acquainted with the teaching about righteousness. But solid food is for the mature, who by constant use have trained themselves to distinguish good from evil. (5:11–14)

Mentoring as intentional discipleship is fundamentally a spiritual matter of drinking and eating. The writer uses this metaphor to compare our spiritual lives of faith to an infant who begins by drinking milk offered by a parent or loved one. An adult, however, cannot physically survive on milk alone. She needs more substance in her diet to sustain her physical body, growth, and development. She must learn to eat on her own or feed herself. At some point, all mature and healthy people will eventually teach others. Likewise, mentoring in our spiritual lives requires a growth in our spiritual diet from milk, to solid food, and eventually to gaining the strength and perseverance to train others to live rightly and distinguish the difference between good and evil.

Let's not be slow to learn regarding the fundamentals of our faith and growth to spiritual maturity. Mentoring fundamentally acquaints us with teachings about righteousness. Like Mandy, we can all be surprised with joy by what we learn on the journey. I led the women's mentoring ministry at my local church, where Mandy attended, for a little over four years. This was not a one-on-one mentoring experience, but rather a community of women working together to build relationships as we intentionally equipped and encouraged each other on our individual faith journeys. In fact, this book was birthed from that experience. Together, we learned how mentoring is pursued out of our passion for God and out of a desire to serve God's people. My desire to mentor was first cultivated during college, where I learned two basic truths about leadership and mentoring:

1. Mentoring is an integral part of leadership; all great leaders mentor.
2. Mentoring is crucial to successfully accomplishing any mission.

Let's consider what these basic principles look like when we approach mentoring as intentional discipleship for God's kingdom purposes. By mentoring for God's purposes, we accept the mission to follow and to fulfill the Great Commission as presented by Jesus in Matthew 28:19–20: "Therefore go and *make disciples* of all nations, baptizing them in the name of the Father and of the Son and of the Holy Spirit, and *teaching them to obey everything I have commanded you*" (emphasis mine). From a biblical perspective, mentoring involves making disciples and teaching those disciples to obey everything Jesus commanded.[7] This is true leadership in action.

Mentoring as intentional discipleship is also about investing in the priorities of God's kingdom and in the lives of other people. It is an intentional approach to discipleship that is progressive first, by inspiring mentees to *know and love God*; second, by helping mentees *understand who they are in Christ*; and finally, by encouraging mentees to *love their neighbors* as they love themselves.[8] This progressive mentoring framework places the whole gospel at center stage and reminds us that the church's most crucial mission is making disciples, which is a serious responsibility for *every* believer.

Mentoring Benefits the Church

Who wouldn't want to join a positive, ever-growing movement that has proven successful? As we reevaluate our definition of mentoring and place it within the context of our biblical understanding, we do not abandon all the practical mentoring skills or best practices learned from marketplace professionals. A quick search of the Harvard Business Review reveals nearly two hundred posts on the topic of mentoring in the workplace. It is common marketplace knowledge that mentoring develops human assets, increases organizational value, and is a crucial component of leadership. This should not surprise us. After all, great leaders mentor!

Mentoring is advocated in the corporate world because it is good for business and it helps the bottom line. Leaders of great corporations identify and train young prodigies with the understanding and hope that their mentees will become the kinds of leaders who take the corporation to the next level. Through teaching, training, modeling, correction, and positive reinforcement, good mentors help their mentees understand their work, make wise decisions, set goals, build teams, and plan strategically. In this way, mentoring develops talent and increases performance so the mentor, mentees, and organizations in which they work and serve are all beneficiaries.

When I consider the resources and programs available in the

business world, I wonder: is the church equally committed to an understanding of mentoring that makes disciples and raises up the next generation of Christian leaders? Whether you are a leader in your church, a stay-at-home mom discipling your children, a Christian working in a professional setting, or simply someone who is frustrated with your church's leadership, this is the book for you, because nurturing Christian leaders of character begins with mentoring. We often miss opportunities to train up leaders in the church because of the misconception that some are leaders— mostly due to their titles, hierarchy, gender, or ordination—and others are not.

This misconception causes many Christians to settle for a complacent life of waiting for someone to tell them what to do, and if no one engages them, they don't act. Mentoring addresses this leadership challenge by making all believers aware of their responsibilities to live on purpose and commit to God's mission. This paradigm shift is a blessing for the church and a means of God's grace to the world. A God-focused and God-purposed mentoring relationship stretches and changes the way we view mentoring *and* leadership alike. *So not only is mentoring a means of intentional discipleship, it is a leadership factory that prepares people of all backgrounds, life stages, and experiences to lead well.*

Embracing mentoring as a leadership factory is wise and crucial for a healthy church. Christ offered a long-term training plan to his disciples, and when he ascended to heaven, leaving them on earth, he commissioned them to work! When leaders are not intentionally training new leaders, the church suffers.

On the other hand, a church can thrive when good leaders are raising up new leaders.[9] The organizations and communities we belong to are constantly growing and changing. Transitions are inevitable. Succession plans are necessary. And for the sake of the mission, we need leaders who are trained and ready to step into a new role at any time.

So what, then, is the purpose of the church, individually and collectively? The Westminster Short Catechism is a good place to begin. It asks the question, "What is the chief end of man?" and then answers, "Man's chief end is to glorify God[10] and enjoy him forever[11]."[12] Glorifying God is the foundational conviction of every true Christian. The commitment to glorify God constantly reminds us that it is God who made us and not we who made ourselves.[13] We are not the masters of our own fates; we are not the captains of our own ships. We are created beings made for the good pleasure of serving our Creator. While God is glorious in and of himself, he has created us to worship him and to fill the earth with his glory.[14] Dr. Tony Evans explains:

> Glory simply means "to be heavy" or "to have weight." It denotes significance. Since all things come from God, are through God, and to God, God's glory exists intrinsically in himself. . . . However, we experience and access that glory when we place ourselves under His comprehensive rule. This is because it is then that God radiates and magnifies His glory to, in, and through us. A primary position for bringing glory to God is that of surrender to His sovereignty. To surrender to God's sovereignty is to acknowledge His jurisdiction, along with the validity of His supremacy, over every area of life.[15]

We humbly glorify God through loving obedience and surrender to his kingdom mission.

Mentoring glorifies God by helping us shift our priorities so Christ can reign supreme over every area of our lives. As followers of Christ, we must all learn to change our priorities, our affections, and the ways we think. Mentoring is a continuous call from confession to repentance (turning around and going in a different direction), and into a passionate pursuit of God. Mentoring as intentional discipleship reminds us that God has a higher purpose for how we think and live. We can daily commit to his way as we "seek first [God's] kingdom and his righteousness" (Matt. 6:33). Only then is our faith truly realized and our dependency on God increased. By seeking God's kingdom first, our personal agendas are replaced, we are released from the bondage of people-pleasing and fulfilling the expectations of others, and we are free to become and do as God intended.

Let's consider the insights of worship leader and author Darlene Zschech:

> It is my deepest desire to remind leaders everywhere that the kingdom of God is about people and that we are not here to build our own kingdoms but to bring God's kingdom into the lives of others. A life lived in Christ is a sacrificial life—a life poured out, a life lived to lift the lives of others.[16]

Mentoring as intentional discipleship allows us to influence others so they forsake the indulgences of this life in exchange for a spirit-filled, life-giving, other-focused existence.

This is your mission. I invite you to take action! We make this mentoring commitment with the declaration that we are God's church, committed to living on purpose and to advancing God's kingdom. Together, we can embody the biblical vision of the Lausanne Movement: "The whole church taking the whole gospel to the whole world."[17] There is no whole church without unity and reconciliation among believers. There is no whole church without the contributions of women, and there is no whole gospel without compassion and justice toward our neighbors. Together, we can change the culture in the church and equip all God's people for service.[18] Will you join this mission?

Mentor for Life

1. How has this chapter changed your understanding of mentoring?

2. Write down any questions you have after reading the chapter and what answers you will seek as you continue reading this book.

3. What is your initial response to the claim that as a Christian, God has called you to mentor others?

4. Mentoring Challenge: Select ten of your friends and family members who are *devoted* Christians (be sure to include people from your local congregation and some from social media with diverse backgrounds) to answer these three questions:

   a. What does it mean to be a disciple of Jesus Christ?

   b. What does it mean to make disciples of Jesus Christ? In your observation, what does that look like?

   c. Do you consistently make disciples? If so, how? If not, why not?

5. Summarize in four or five sentences what you have learned from this chapter.

Tweet This

"Mentoring is about intentionally investing in the priorities of God's kingdom and in the lives of others." #Mentor4Life @asistasjourney

Two

Connect Evangelism and Discipleship

*Evangelism is more than getting people to change their
individual lifestyle or convincing them to convert to Christ.
It is about inviting them to join God's family and to join
forces with what God is doing in the world.*

Dr. Brenda Salter McNeil[1]

As I boarded the big airplane heading to Newport, Rhode Island,
for the start of military training at the Naval Academy Preparatory
School, I was afraid. Until that moment, I had been a confident
young lady secure in her life pursuits and successes, but I was now
keenly aware of my fragility. My mom and dad, my anchors of
support, were not boarding that plane with me. I was a young
black girl from South Carolina going to an elite, predominately
white, male-dominated school—a school rigorous in both its academic and military instruction. It would be cold, lonely, and many
miles from home. Sure, there would be designated opportunities
for students to call their families on the public hallway pay phones
(very few people had cell phones at the time), but that would not
be the same as the comfort of my mom's hugs or my dad's kisses.
Those brief calls would not provide the nurturing support and

encouragement I was accustomed to. I was scared and knew I needed something more.

At the time, I did not have a relationship with Christ, but having been raised in the church, I had enough sense to call on him for help. So I boarded the plane and mentally rattled off a quick prayer:

Dear God, I need you. I don't know what to do. I'm going off into this big world all alone. Please protect me. If you do, Lord, I will serve you with my life. Amen.

I threw my bag in the overhead bin, sat down, and listened to Kirk Franklin's tune, *More Than Conquerors*, on my portable CD player:

> *We ran the race, we kept the fight.*
> *We shed our blood for what was right.*
> *We carried our cross through storm and rain.*
> *Because of Christ, now we can say, "We are conquerors."*

The lyrics seemed appropriate. I put the song on repeat and thought about what it might mean to really *know* Jesus personally, for myself.

After endless Sunday mornings in church, countless prayers, and multiple baptisms (I was both sprinkled and immersed), I still could not answer that awful question, "If I died today, would I go to heaven?" Perhaps all the trappings of church were supposed to reassure me, but deep inside, I still wasn't sure. Although many people had talked to me about Jesus, no one in my first eighteen years of life had ever offered to intentionally disciple me. Apart from references to the followers of Jesus in the Bible, the word *discipleship* was rarely heard from the lips of the professing Christians I knew. I was just another willfully sinful, professing Christian who went to church and did good works. I knew about Jesus, but I couldn't honestly consider myself one of his followers—a disciple.

By the world's standards, I was a "good" person, and yet there was no doubt in my mind that I was spiritually lost. I wondered, shouldn't Christians be different? Are we faithful in our evangelistic practices if we are only asking people whether they have given their hearts to Jesus, or whether they are going to heaven? I don't know what your spiritual journey has been like, and I don't know the questions you have right now, but if you have picked up this book, that tells me you are wrestling and searching for answers of some kind. That's a good thing!

I believe we must contemplate the important need for mentoring and discipleship in light of a closely related issue: evangelism. How do we think about evangelism today? Do we, as Christians, care about the lost among us? Do we understand the urgency of the gospel? And are we willing to do whatever it takes to make Jesus' name known among those in our areas of influence?[2] Let's probe these questions together.

Evangelism in America

When I'm asked to describe my religious views, I quickly respond, "I am an evangelical."[3] Simply stated, that means I believe Jesus is both fully God and fully man. He is the gateway to a meaningful personal relationship with the one and only true and living God.[4] The Bible is the true and inspired Word of God, which states, "If you declare with your mouth, 'Jesus is Lord,' and believe in your heart that God raised him from the dead, you will be saved. For it is with your heart that you believe and are justified, and it is with your mouth that you profess your faith and are saved" (Rom. 10:9–10). As an evangelical, I am compelled to share this good news that while we were sinners, Christ died for us (Rom. 5:8).

Are you a lover of God's Word? Wouldn't it be appropriate to observe what the New Testament reveals about evangelism and discipleship? The Bible does reveal good news, but not just so people can say an empty "prayer of salvation." In the Gospels, we observe needy people coming to Jesus because they are desperate. He offers healing to the sick and hope for the weary, all the while evaluating the hearts of individuals, forgiving their sins, and calling them unto himself. The invitation was always to *follow him*. The exciting thing is that people found out about this Savior through the words and testimonies of their friends and family.[5] This is how the kingdom is ushered in. This is how lives are changed, and this is how God's mission gets accomplished in the world. How does it make you feel to know that God is pleased to have you share the good news and to invite others to join in his kingdom work?

As you consider this invitation, let's try to develop a sense of urgency and devotion concerning the sacred call to mentor. These first few chapters are written in the hope that they will usher you toward this goal. I have a deep concern that far too often, we ask people to say a prayer of salvation to a God they don't even know, and we do this without giving them sufficient opportunity to consider the gravity or the cost of their decision to follow Christ.

Let's take a look at what this cost means to our Christian brothers and sisters in other parts of the world. What truths about evangelism can we learn from them? In her book *A Credible Witness*, Dr. Brenda Salter McNeil writes about a conversation she had with two young evangelists in Singapore:

> [They] would never expect a person to make a life-changing decision to accept and follow Jesus Christ on the same night the gospel was first preached to them. In fact, they would be suspicious of anyone who made a decision like that too hastily. It would indicate that the person had not thought carefully enough about the risks and the costliness of their decision, that they hadn't soberly considered the possible price they might have to pay, like being disowned by their family, ostracized from their community, or beaten or killed for their faith. Instead of encouraging a potential convert to come to the altar, they would counsel that person to wait and go home

to really think about all the ramifications before they made a firm decision. If after an extended period of personal reflection and soul searching they still wanted to accept Jesus Christ as their Lord and Savior, they would then be invited to do so.[6]

These brothers in Christ are echoing the words of Jesus, who taught his hearers to consider the cost of being his disciple.[7] You see, following Jesus is not a decision to be taken lightly. It includes a call to repentance and our willingness to be changed by him. Are we willing to put Jesus first? Are we willing to make him Savior *and* Lord of our lives—even if we have to walk away from our family, culture, community, work, and *everything* that has become comfortable for us? I begin with the perspective of these brothers from Singapore, not to discount those who have come to Christ after saying a "prayer of salvation" and have remained faithful to that confession throughout their personal lives, but rather to broaden our understanding concerning evangelism and discipleship.

Our Old Way of Doing Things

Our predominant cultural method of evangelism typically means that someone preaches the Word, asks new converts to say a prayer of salvation, and then gives those converts a charge to go to church, pray, and read their Bibles every day. In the Gospels, Jesus taught another way of evangelism that may be even more meaningful to us at this crucial time in church history. He taught that evangelism cannot be separated from the call to discipleship. They go together.

The call to discipleship means new relationships of faith must be forged, with sound teaching, real accountability, and consistent follow-up after the initial prayer.

The Christian faith can be discouraging to new believers who may sincerely attempt to pray and even go to church for a season, but then return to their old lives, their same jobs, and their same friends. Their faith and their lives ultimately remain separate, which is not what Jesus intended. When this kind of separation continues, new believers struggle. In reality, they have not had a miraculous encounter with the Lord. Their hearts have not been changed. Like me, they may have been raised in a religious environment, even said a prayer or gone through the motions, but they are still spiritually lost. The church has not given them what they truly need to move forward as disciples of Christ. Because you love them and desire God's best for their lives, you can offer a new way of doing things.

Robert E. Coleman, author of *The Master Plan of Evangelism*, shares this concern. He writes, "When will the church learn this lesson? Preaching to the masses, although necessary, will never suffice in the work of preparing leaders for evangelism. Nor can *occasional* prayer meetings and training classes for Christian workers do this job. Building men and women is *not* that easy. It requires *constant personal attention*, much like a father gives to his children"[8] (emphasis mine). The solution to this problem is constant personal attention in the church. We cannot continue to leave our spiritual infants to fend for themselves. We cannot be apathetic toward the lost, immature, sick, lonely, and brokenhearted among us. As a family, all our members need personal care.

I realize I am not the first to address this. In an effort to find a solution, some local churches may offer confirmation or convocation courses that are either associated with baptism or new church membership. Or they may offer numerous short-term Bible studies, but ongoing opportunities for spiritual growth, leadership training, and discipleship are limited. And while I would never discount the importance of Bible study, acquiring biblical knowledge is not the same as learning to follow Jesus. Jesus himself was the perfect living Word, and even he understood that people needed more than his words alone. They needed an ongoing relationship with him. They needed his constant correction, and they needed to follow him as he served others. New believers need this as well—they need examples of what it means to be a real, flesh-and-blood follower of Jesus:

> Unless new Christians . . . have parents or friends who will fill the gap [between the "prayer of salvation" and their growth to a place of spiritual maturity] in a real way, they are often left entirely on their own to find solutions to the innumerable practical problems confronting their lives, any one of which could mean disaster for their new faith. With such haphazard follow-up by the church, it is no wonder that about half of those who make professions and join the church eventually fall away or lose the glow of the salvation experience, and fewer still grow in sufficient knowledge and grace to be of any real service to the kingdom.[9]

Can we please agree to stop championing a method of evangelism that fails to disciple believers into spiritual maturity? Over the past decade, I've become convinced that we can rectify this error through mentoring as intentional discipleship. Mentoring helps us build trustworthy relationships as we partner with God through the transformational work of the Holy Spirit to change hearts and minds. Mentoring makes the connection between evangelism and discipleship. My friends, we need this connection.

Through mentoring, we disciple people *unto* salvation. In other words, we are all a work in progress. God is the one who draws people in, as we see throughout the New Testament. And yet that is not the end—it is only the beginning. Through mentoring, we invite people to "taste and see that the LORD is good" (Ps. 34:8). Once they have tasted, they must be taught how to eat. They need to learn how to faithfully partake of his goodness and grace so they can continue to grow in faith. And as they grow, we invite them to extend the same grace they have received by mentoring others. Mentoring leads to multiplication.

Making Disciples in a Pluralistic World

During an interview with Dr. Howard-John Wesley, senior pastor of the historic Alfred Street Baptist Church in Alexandria, Virginia, I asked, "What are some of the internal challenges facing the black church today?" One of his responses is applicable not just to the black church, but to the American church at large. It is also significant as we consider the challenges of discipleship. He said, "We must create Christians who have a broad worldview and understand their role as Christians in a pluralistic society. In other words, we need to challenge Christians to live out the Christian principle of 'love for all' while still proclaiming the biblical truth that salvation is found in Christ alone."[10]

As disciples, this is our current evangelistic challenge. We live in an ever-changing world, but Christ was never afraid to confront worldly issues. He entered into the messiness of people's lives. We must be willing to follow his example. This means paying attention and knowing what is happening in the culture around us. It means having a proper context for engaging in the lives of those we are blessed to influence. It is essential that we understand that not everyone comes to the mentoring relationship—or to the church, for that matter—with the same convictions, same knowledge, education, life experiences, family heritage, traditions, and backgrounds we have. Before we tell potential mentees what we think they need, we should get to know them and try to understand where they are and from where they have come.

Many elements shape the heart and mind of a person, and as mentors seeking to disciple others, we can begin by training ourselves to listen, to pay attention to what's going on in the world and how it impacts people's lives, and then ask our mentees some probing questions, like "What do you think about this?" or "Why do you feel that way?" Questions like these can lead to intimate teaching moments, and that's exactly what Jesus did with his own disciples. The "new" approach to evangelism and discipleship is not really new at all. It's a return to the basics, to the ways of Jesus.

On the Journey with Jesus

The four Gospels document the life and earthly ministry of Jesus. Each of them records the miracle of Jesus feeding five thousand men, plus numerous women and children, with only five fish and two loaves of bread.[11] I'd like to examine this scene in the four Gospels. This method, if you haven't done it before, is kind of like watching the making of a movie through four different camera lenses. I believe we can learn about mentoring through the intimate exchanges between Jesus and his disciples that led up to the miracle. Pay attention to how Jesus engages his culture, his community, and his disciples. I believe this reveals how mentoring can be an effective tool for evangelism.

The Setting: late in the evening in a far-off place. For everyone in the scene, it has been a long day.

Characters: Jesus, the twelve disciples, and a crowd of needy people.

Plot: Jesus is tired, hungry, and in mourning. We know he is tired because the scene begins with him drawing away with his twelve disciples for the purpose of rest. We know he is hungry because everyone else is hungry, and it is unlikely that his conscience would allow him to eat while those around him are wanting. Matthew and Mark record that Jesus is also mourning the death of his relative, John the Baptist, whom he loved and respected. Everybody who has ever lost a loved one knows grief makes your body tired. In addition to the news of John's death, Jesus' weary condition may also be attributed to his leadership and unwavering commitment to sharing God's mission and message. Mark and Luke record that he was receiving reports from the apostles about their ministry assignments. People were coming and going around him throughout the day. That's tiring. Additionally, John records that prior to this scene, Jesus was healing people, and we know from the story of the "Woman with the Issue of Blood," Jesus felt strength depart from him when he healed a person.[12]

The arrival of a crowd at this remote location does not give Jesus the time he needs to rest. Both Matthew and Mark record that *Jesus has compassion on them*. Luke writes that he welcomes them. Because they are like sheep without a shepherd, he begins teaching them about the kingdom of God. Because some are sick, he heals them. He continues to minister throughout the day and well into the evening hours.

Maybe the disciples just can't take it anymore, or perhaps they hear grumblings in the crowd, but the need for food becomes a pressing concern. Physical hunger is what generates conflict in this story. Let us not forget that the crowds left their towns to follow Jesus and hear his teaching. Mark writes that the people "ran on foot" to get to Jesus. These are not the days of Gatorade, energy drinks, and electrolyte replenishments. Additionally, many of these people were traveling with children. It is likely that the children were tired, thirsty, hungry, and restless at the point of their arrival, but that did not stop them from running after and sitting at the feet of Jesus all day and into the evening hours. When their aching bellies can hold out no longer, the disciples say to Jesus, "Send them away to get something to eat."

How does Jesus reply? He gives them an impossible assignment: "You give them something to eat" (Mark 6:37).

To grasp the power of this simple statement, we must look more closely at the gospel of John. Jesus asks Philip, "Where shall we buy bread for these people to eat?" (John 6:5). The author writes, "[Jesus] asked this only to test him, for he already had in mind what he was going to do" (John 6:6). In other words, this assignment is only a test. Jesus knows he is asking more than is possible.

How does this apply to our commission to make disciples? As we minister to others, Jesus places people in our lives who are hungry, tired, spiritually thirsty, sick, and in need of healing. He knows we, too, are hungry, that we need to eat, and so we must also work. He knows we mourn the disappointments and losses in our own lives. He understands when we are tired and need rest. Yet he still calls us to serve. To feed those in need. This can bring us to the end of ourselves. It is a test of our faith. It requires us to reach out beyond our skills, gifts, and resources to depend upon Jesus and the work of his Spirit. It requires humility. Amid the realities of our lives, Jesus asks, *When I bring someone who is needy before you, will you put all your cares aside and have compassion on her?*

Jesus understood that true ministry is holistic; it includes nourishment for the body *and* the soul, and that's part of the message he was teaching his disciples. But he was also teaching them that he is more than able to supply what they need to minister effectively to lost people. The undercurrent of this story, and his message to us, can be summarized in three words: *faith, hope,* and *love. Faith* is needed to follow Jesus, *hope* reminds us of what Christ can do with lost people who come to him, but the greatest of all that we can do for people is to *love* them.[13] Love for Christ and love of others is the driving force of mentoring; it births compassion in our hearts and compels us to action. So when we consider mentoring as intentional discipleship, let us be compelled by love—our love for God and our love for other people.

Mentor for Life

1. Prior to reading this chapter, what was your understanding of evangelism and its connection to discipleship? What were some of your approaches to evangelism, and what was your follow-up commitment to discipleship?

2. Why does it sometimes seem like there is no real difference between the lives of professing Christians and those who are lost in the world?

3. Make a list of three people God might be leading you to mentor. Begin praying for them as you continue reading this book.

4. How can the concept of mentoring help you connect your prior understanding of evangelism and the current call to make disciples?

5. Summarize in four or five sentences what you have learned from this chapter.

Tweet This

"Love for Christ and love of others is the driving force of mentoring. It births compassion in our hearts." #Mentor4Life @asistasjourney

Three

Shape Culture and the Church

*One of the most important functions of Christian prophets in
our day is the ability to perceive the consequences of various
forces in our culture and to make value judgments upon them.*
Richard J. Foster[1]

Sometimes life seems like one big interruption. Considering our communication systems and technological advancements, we spend most of our days being interrupted. Interruptions come in the form of Facebook updates, Twitter notifications, vibrating cell phones, and emails arriving in our in-boxes. Then, of course, there are the distractions of people walking into our cubicles as we attempt to work, or children barging into their parents' bedrooms unannounced, or the dear friend who requests help at the last minute because "something came up" (something always comes up). We live in a society where everything is urgent and people constantly demand our immediate attention.

Some of these attention-grabbers are telling us things about God, our lives, our priorities, and how to engage the world. We receive messages all day long about ourselves, telling us what's most important and how to live. Some of them are from marketing campaigns designed to influence our purchases or garner our votes of approval. Commercials, news articles, our favorite television shows, friends on social media—all of these are targeting us, competing for our attention, speaking to our desires, and telling us how to think.

These interruptions play into our attitudes and approaches to discipleship by allowing our overindulgent, me-centered American culture to determine what we prioritize in church ministry. We need to look at our lives and ask, *Does God really have our attention, or is he just another interruption?* Are we actually applying God's messages to our lives or simply going with the flow of the culture? Making disciples requires that we consciously challenge people about their priorities, teaching them how to filter the messages they receive according to God's standards.

The Influence of Culture

My husband entered Marine Corps boot camp as an eighteen-year-old boy, thirteen days after high school graduation. Military indoctrination included immersion into the culture of the Marine Corps. We both entered the military *before* it transitioned to the digital camouflage uniforms (which Marines don't have to iron) and the suede military boots (which Marines do not polish), so one of the key parts of our indoctrination into the culture was the simple practice of ironing uniforms and polishing boots. This regular discipline became a means of bonding with those who embarked on the military journey with us. In fact, much of our "indoctrination" into the military way of life was made up of simple shifts in the way we lived. It was those countless hours devoted to developing little disciplines, as well as a sense that what we were doing was different from the rest of the world's standards, that began to make us into Marines. We took pride in the way we presented ourselves, and we intentionally cultivated our minds to become Marines.

We also entered the military during a time when recruits and officer candidates did not have access to telephones, television, the internet, media, or any outside source for at least six weeks. So during those six weeks of initial indoctrination, we were conditioned to learn a new culture and embrace a new way of life. My husband went from being called "Corey" to being known as "Recruit Robinson." I went from being called "Tasha" (the nickname given me by my close family and friends) to being "Midshipman Candidate Sistrunk." In this new culture, no one cared about our first names, our previous accomplishments, or our family histories. They only knew us as sailors and marines. We were part of a new family, the military family. In this new family, we learned to value the military unit—our shared community—above our individual abilities, rights, and needs. Our character was shaped to conform to military standards and expectations. We were constantly challenged to evaluate our old thoughts and old ways of life. When we weren't working hard together, we were memorizing regulations, ironing uniforms, and polishing shoes.

In the Marines, the simple daily choices we made over a consistent period of time were what changed us. If we embraced the changes, we thrived and our family members and friends witnessed the transformation when they saw us at the end of that indoctrination period. I share this because it is a vivid illustration of what real discipleship looks like. If we are to truly follow Christ, we must reject the world's standards and cultural expectations, exchanging them for a new way of living and being.

When I speak of culture in this book, I typically mean all things American—apple pie with vanilla ice cream, pledging allegiance to the flag, and the values of democracy and capitalism. The Constitution shapes American culture, as do the major players of society (i.e., those with money, power, and respect). American culture values life (at least in most instances), liberty, and the pursuit of happiness, which includes the pursuit of the coveted modern version of the American dream. And finally, our culture determines how we define success.

Yet it isn't just the big players—the government, the media, entertainers, and the corporate world—that shape culture. Grassroots efforts like the women's liberation and civil rights movements also remind us that culture is shaped by the attitudes of regular people like you and me. It is both a top-down *and* a bottom-up phenomenon.

What does American culture value? Our culture values, above all else, the *individual's right* to pursue his or her dreams, and therefore, our lives are often self-seeking and extremely competitive. Pastor and author David Platt writes about the influence of the American dream on our Christian faith:

> The dangerous assumption we unknowingly accept in the American dream is that our greatest asset is our own ability. The American dream prizes what people can accomplish when they believe in themselves and trust in themselves, and we are drawn toward such thinking. But the gospel has different priorities. The gospel beckons us to die to ourselves and to believe in God and to trust in his power.[2]

Mentoring necessarily addresses where we have put our hopes and dreams. It helps us to realize that God's standards are in direct contrast to our American culture. As children, we are indoctrinated in our homes, community, and school systems into certain ways of thinking. We develop a specific worldview. And until it is brought to our attention, we don't even realize the cultural messages that have taken root in our hearts to shape our decision-making and our actions.

I think about this often when I'm wrestling with questions about the Christian response to injustice throughout history. One of my professors, Dr. Donald Fairbairn, Professor of Early Christianity at Gordon-Conwell Theological Seminary in Charlotte, North Carolina, reminded me that we are all products of our time. He said:

We often speak of "the Christian worldview," but we also need to recognize that any given Christian's personal worldview is going to be a mixture of the values of the gospel and the values of the society in which he or she lives. Few Christians think rigorously about the difference between the Christian worldview and their cultural worldview. Most Christians simply absorb the values they are exposed to, whether those come ultimately from the gospel or the prevailing society. In fact, when a given society's culture has been influenced a lot by Christianity (as is the case in America), it is especially easy for people to assume that cultural values are the same as Christian values, and so they fail to think deeply about the cases where the culture has gone astray.[3]

Our culture has gone astray; therefore, part of mentoring others as disciples of Jesus includes training them to respond to the fallen world's culture in a healthy way. For those of us who are excited about living our lives on purpose for God, there is good news about cultural influence. In his book, *Culture Making: Recovering Our Creative Calling*, author Andy Crouch shares that Christians tend to respond to culture in one of four ways: condemnation, critique, copying, or consuming. Condemning culture means we talk among ourselves and mutually agree about how bad things are becoming. This yields little to no cultural effect.[4] We see this condemnation happening when Christians enter political discussions and debates, emphasizing their own views and perspectives rather than engaging the broader culture.

Critiquing culture means we do not condemn our culture outright; rather, we carefully analyze it to reveal its inadequacies where it is misguided.[5] Much of our online Christian media consists of this kind of dialog. Copying culture goes a step further. We copy culture whenever we imitate or replace what we perceive as offensive with what Christians may consider more reasonable or pleasant.[6] In my opinion, a negative example of this practice is the rise of reality television shows being marketed to Christians, many of which are no more tasteful than their secular counterparts. Finally, some Christians choose to consume culture more carefully, sometimes selectively or strategically. As consumers, we unwittingly become part of the problem because our choices "have undeniable power in shaping what is produced."[7]

Through mentoring as intentional discipleship, we learn there is a fifth way, a gospel-centered way to respond to our culture. Andy Crouch writes, *"The only way to change culture is to create more of it. . . .* cultural change will only happen when something new displaces, to some extent, existing culture in a very tangible way."[8] By identifying these various ways of engaging culture, Crouch is not advocating for a new way of living for Christ in a lost world. He is adequately, eloquently, and artistically articulating what God originally intended for all humanity and what Jesus now purposes for us, his redeemed people.

Cultural redemption can be the beautiful product of a united, kingdom-minded church that prioritizes discipleship. But it will only happen when we bring the truth of the gospel to bear on the values of our culture and challenge ourselves to think deeply about our own values and the areas where American culture has gone astray, especially when the church has followed suit. When Christians don't wrestle deeply with the values of culture *and how they differ from the gospel*, we will inevitably be more influenced by the culture than by God's purpose and plans for the body of Christ.

Living in America: Culture Shaping and the Church

What do these cultural challenges and opportunities mean for the church? Since American culture is both a top-down *and* a bottom-up phenomenon, we should not be surprised to find that it shapes the American church and the hearts of individuals within the church. When Christian leaders confidently declare, "We have a healthy church" or "We have a successful ministry," I often wonder, "How are you determining that?" In many churches, ministry success is attached to the pastor's charisma and leadership, membership and/or weekly attendance numbers, or the size of their building and budget. It might be based on the number of visitors or baptisms on any given Sunday. And while there is some value in knowing these metrics, do we really believe they are the primary means to assess ministry effectiveness? We must exercise great caution whenever we measure church success by American cultural standards. If we are asking the wrong questions, we will chart the wrong course forward in our churches.

David Platt addresses this problem at length in his New York Times bestseller *Radical: Taking Back Your Faith from the American Dream*. In discussing the need for discipleship, he highlights many of the blind spots of American Christianity. Platt points out that we seek a false sense of security in the things of this world. He calls attention to our lack of urgency for missions and how we incorrectly assume that a call to Christianity is a call to comfortable living.[9] These are all crucial challenges to discipleship, and Platt provides an excellent examination of those topics, so we will not revisit them here. I will, however, offer another cultural challenge I frequently see in the church today: our insatiable desire to have choices.

The grocery store has almost endless options if you want to buy, say, breakfast cereal, or even a bottle of water. Seriously, it's water in a plastic bottle. How many choices do we need? This is just one example indicative of how market competition has created in us a wider cultural expectation of endless choices. This is a problem because we incorrectly conclude that we should be able to expect an endless number of choices everywhere. The same people who encounter almost limitless possibilities in their grocery store aisles or on their restaurant menus develop an expectation that the church will feed their personal appetites, which can change from day to day. Because church and ministry leaders live in the very same culture, our knee-jerk reaction is to accommodate every one of these "needs" and add yet another ministry to the list whenever a new need is expressed. The result is that quantity trumps quality.

And since offering more ministries means more volunteers are needed to sustain them, before anyone knows it, the faithful few are busy *doing* at the expense of *being* present with God. In most cases, this behavior leads to burnout, and instead of the church offering a resting place of worship that beckons souls to draw near to the Lord, it simply adds weight to the over-productive lives of its congregants. The modern church constantly develops new programs, ministries, and activities, all of which present new challenges. But for all of these ministry options and choices, the fruit of the modern church is not always growing disciples of Christ. Instead, the church has become a tree that produces busy, distracted laypeople lacking spiritual depth and maturity.

In their book *The Critical Journey*, authors Janet O. Hagberg and Robert A. Guelich define the fruit of our ministry efforts today as the "productive stage." It's what happens when the focus of our faith becomes performance-based and we (as individuals and congregations) subtly become more self-focused and less focused on God and others. Our various areas of ministry service become a means of evaluating our self-worth and shamelessly fulfilling unmet needs in our own hearts:

> Feeling almost invincible, we are led in lock-step progression to playing God in our own life and in the lives of others. . . . The harder we work, the more success we have, the stronger our faith must be. We put our desires in the place of God and call it God's will. And if challenged, we will deny it vehemently, frequently using Scripture or other evidence to prove us right. . . . We strive so hard to be loved for what we have done rather than for who we are. We are ultimately very, very lonely people.[10]

And so we can see how following our indulgences, trying to live a "do good," performance-based life, and chasing worldly measures of success causes us to miss the bigger picture of what God really wants to do in and through us. Platt writes:

> What is strangely lacking in the picture of performances, personalities, programs, and professionals is desperation for the power of God. God's power is at best an add-on to our strategies. I am frightened by the reality that the church I lead can carry on most of our activities smoothly, efficiently, even successfully, never realizing that the Holy Spirit of God is virtually absent from the picture. We can so easily deceive ourselves, mistaking the presence of physical bodies in a crowd for the existence of spiritual life in a community.[11]

Against this culturally conditioned Christianity, the call to mentoring as intentional discipleship invites us to experience spiritual life in community with others. This will naturally conflict with an American church philosophy that measures the success of ministries or congregations simply by how fast they grow. As my academic advisor has reminded many seminary students heading out to serve in churches, "Weeds grow, but that doesn't make them healthy." Rather than focusing on numerical growth, we must first evaluate the conditions of our hearts, and the primary question for consideration should always be, "How are we making disciples of Jesus Christ?" By beginning there, we better prioritize the focus of our local congregations and ministries, and thus, we better impact the culture and serve the world.

Cultural Change and Where the American Church Needs to Pay Attention

For much of this chapter, I've tried to provide a snapshot of how we, as the church in America, have compromised and missed our calling to make disciples. But I believe the twenty-first century is a crucial time in church history. The world around us is ever-changing. In America, we are seeing dramatic shifts in moral values, political systems, and ethnic makeup. The racial and ethnic dynamics will drastically change in America over the next thirty years, and whites will no longer be the majority.[12] This is crucial for "most mainline churches in the United States . . . [which] have congregations that are nearly entirely white."[13] Additionally, Millennials are leaving churches at an alarming rate. Some do not find purpose in the traditional church.[14] These cultural realities indicate some of the future challenges we will face. We need to look at ourselves honestly and confess that in spite of the large number of churches we still see today, the American church generally:

- Lacks biblical literacy among laypeople[15]
- Lacks servant, competent, and courageous leadership[16]
- Lacks intentionality in tapping women as vital resources in the church[17]
- Lacks unity within the universal church, particularly in the areas of denominational division, generational divides, and racial reconciliation[18]

While many local congregations intentionally confront these challenges, collectively we are suffering. The solution, I would suggest, is *not* to seek relevance by offering different services, gimmicks, charismatic speakers, and endless programming. The solution is to return to our core mission of making disciples. Only then can we turn these potential community risks into future opportunities to influence culture and advance God's kingdom.

Mentor for Life

1. How do you measure success in your workplace, church ministry, family, and life? How do you think God defines success in those areas? Why do you believe this is true?

2. Our American culture deceives us into thinking we do not have enough [fill in the blank]. Do you sometimes find yourself getting caught in the trap of feeling like you don't have enough? How does the reality that three billion people live on less than two U.S. dollars a day[19] change your perspective of what you "want" versus what you "need"? How does this impact the way you approach the needs of others or the missional and ministry needs of the universal church?

3. In your current life and ministry context, how are you now making disciples of Jesus Christ?

4. As you contemplate the need for mentoring, how have the issues raised in this chapter challenged you?

5. Summarize in four or five sentences what you have learned from this chapter.

Tweet This

"Cultural redemption can be a beautiful
consequence of a united church that prioritizes
discipleship." #Mentor4Life @asistasjourney

If you are planting for a year, plant grain.
If you are planting for a decade, plant trees.
If you are planting for a century, plant people.
Chinese Proverb

In the summer of 2002, I began my Marine Corps Officer Training in Quantico, Virginia, by receiving a core "issue" of uniforms and several crucial items to fill my sea. For six months, I hiked around with a backpack that weighed approximately 85 percent of my body weight. With the other new officers, I stayed up long hours, ran many miles, and lifted lots of weights. I did things I wasn't sure my body and mind were capable of doing. Together, as a unit, we completed all sorts of military training and spent several days in the field, sometimes in the rain, snow, and ice. Whether we were sleep deprived, food deprived, or tear gassed, we continued our training. The other new officers, my peers, came from all walks of life, but we always learned as a team. Early on, it was ingrained into our psyches that "Marines win battles. And battles win wars." We believed we were the world's finest fighting machine, that if any enemy came up against us, we would have victory, but gaining that victory meant we must first be prepared to fight!

These military lessons have helped me better understand the spiritual battles raging all around us. They have also motivated me where training and preparation for mentoring are concerned. As disciples of Christ, we have been delegated spiritual authority in the world, and we can depend on each other when the Enemy of our souls comes against us with his attacks. When in a spiritual war, we need confidence in God—our commander and King—and in the power, knowledge, and tools he has provided to ensure our victory.

As Christians, we need to understand that we are living in two kingdoms, and while our allegiance is to only one of them, we have responsibilities in both. We live in the kingdom of this world where our Enemy, the Devil, has limited reign (Eph. 2:1–2). He walks around the earth like a roaring lion seeking people to destroy (1 Pet. 5:8). Yet we are also citizens of a heavenly kingdom (Phil. 3:20) where God sits on his throne and rules from on high. This is the kingdom Jesus spoke about and ushered in. This is the kingdom he prayed would reveal his Father's will on earth as it is in heaven.

God reigned in heaven and on earth from the very beginning. When God created Adam, he breathed his own breath or Spirit into Adam to give him life (Gen. 2:7). Initially, he created Adam to work in the garden (Gen. 2:4–8). Then he created Adam's wife, Eve, and together gave them the command to "be fruitful and increase in number; fill the earth and subdue it" (Gen. 1:28). God continued by charging them to "rule over" earth's creatures, and gave them "seed-bearing" plants and fruit trees with *seeds* in them. With these commands, God clearly communicated that he had every intention for man and woman to cultivate their environment, to cause everything they touched to grow and produce to the glory of God. When God made humans in his own image (Gen. 1:26), he assumed his presence and reign would be reflected on earth and impact every aspect of their lives. From the creation passages and the cultural mandate of Genesis 1:26–30, we know God's glory is revealed through our flourishing and multiplication.

Once sin entered the world (Gen. 3), however, it led to division. Humans were separated from God, the rest of creation, and each other, and it became clear that someone else was also trying to multiply his image and his influence in the world. The garden of Eden is where Satan launched his spiritual battle against human beings, and ultimately against God. Though we exist as physical beings, we must acknowledge immortal beings that are either angelic or demonic. Both sides understand the warring kingdoms and conflict between what God wants and what Satan wants. We must understand that these spiritual beings and kingdom warriors defend their respective kings and do not quit.

George Barna writes, "Even though [our] battle record is incidental to the ultimate outcome, each side makes a play for [our] allegiance as if its success depended upon winning [us] over. Every moment of every day we are at war."[1] The reality of this spiritual war affects us all and has the potential to destroy us if we don't understand our identity in Christ. No wonder Paul admonished the Corinthians by calling them ambassadors for Christ (2 Cor. 5:20). He was reminding them who they represented and whose side they were on.

Jesus understood the temptations of culture and the magnitude of spiritual warfare. Immanuel became like us and lived through the tensions we experience in this world. "For we do not have a high priest [Christ] who is unable to empathize with our weaknesses, but we have one who has been tempted in every way, just as we are—yet he did not sin. Let us then approach God's throne of grace with confidence, so that we may receive mercy and find grace to help us in our time of need" (Heb. 4:15–16). Jesus is our present help in this spiritual battle. As the one who calls people to discipleship, he understands God's kingdom as it relates to the kingdom of this world, and how to teach and prepare disciples to live out God's purposes in this fallen world at war. As those called to mentor on mission for God, we also need this crucial warfare intelligence.

The Kingdom of Man

The cultural mandate, as it is commonly called, is to "be fruitful and increase in number" (Gen. 1:28). This command was given to Adam and Eve at creation and is directly connected to the Great Commission of Christ to "make disciples" (Matt. 28:19). So how does this mandate connect with mentoring as intentional discipleship? I believe we effectively prepare for spiritual battles by mentoring and multiplying in the same way Jesus did with his disciples. We faithfully gather with a small group of people and, through teaching and practice, mentor them to follow Jesus. Through mentoring, we grow in our love and understanding of God, self, and others. We learn the foundational and sustaining tenets of the Christian faith, and our purpose and calling is clarified. Then we train and equip mentees to win in their daily battles and to mentor others who will follow Jesus. By creating disciples, we intentionally take this victorious gospel message that would have been stagnant, and we spread it all over the earth through both our words and our deeds. Essentially, the gospel-centered way to respond to a fallen world and an infected culture is *to create—to make more disciples who live on purpose for God's kingdom and give them the charge to lead others who do the same*. We proactively take a stand against our Enemy by mentoring and multiplying.

Upon entering the gates of the U.S. Naval Academy, all plebes (freshmen) are issued a pocket-sized book called *Reef Points*. It includes everything you need to know to survive Plebe Summer (freshman basic training). This plebe dictionary features The 27 Laws of the Navy, some of which we memorize. The Fifth Law of the Navy reads like a Scripture from the King James translation:

On the strength of one link in the cable, Dependeth the might of the chain, Who knows when thou mayest be tested? So live that thou bearest the strain![2] This law teaches us that a cable is only as strong as its weakest link. It is a humble reminder that as a team, we are only as strong as our weakest member. Our training required times of testing so we could learn to bear the strain together.

This is another example of how military lessons have had important implications for my spiritual growth. You see, nobody wants to be the weakest link in the cable. Yet weak links are inevitable when we form relationships in the church. So how do we treat those who are weaker, who lack understanding, who don't realize they are in the midst of a spiritual war, who struggle and aren't quite where we think they should be? The apostle Paul teaches that weak links are people worthy of our honor (1 Cor. 12:22–23). Weak links are those who have been beaten up by Satan or his demons, swallowed up by culture, hurt in the church, or disillusioned by our ineffective evangelistic practices. Weak links should not be left for dead. Weak links need embracing, refinement, and strengthening. Weak links need a clear picture of these high stakes, weak links need lots of love, and weak links need discipleship. Instead of judgment and rejection, the commitment to mentoring conditions the entire body of Christ to stand strong together and bear the strain of living for Christ in this fallen world. In the kingdom of man, we stand strongest when we stand together.

The Kingdom of God

The kingdom of God has defeated the kingdom of Satan, and each day, that victory is enacted in the lives of individual people God is saving from the grip of the Enemy. Hallelujah! The book of Colossians affirms our victory by articulating the supremacy of Christ:

> God made you alive with Christ. He forgave us all our sins,
> having canceled the charge of our legal indebtedness, which
> stood against us and condemned us; he has taken it away,
> nailing it to the cross. And having disarmed the powers and
> authorities, he made a public spectacle of them, triumphing
> over them by the cross. (Col. 2:13–15).

It is the finished work of Christ on the cross that affirms our identity. Christ's blood is the proof that we belong to God, and when we pledge our allegiance to his kingdom, the power of the Holy Spirit changes our hearts and transforms our lives. The blood of Jesus breaks our bondage from Satan's kingdom and gives us the power to live a new life in Christ. Through Christ, we live for God with his heavenly kingdom in view. Dr. Tony Evans writes:

> Let's connect the truth of our salvation to the purpose we are
> called to live. Our purpose in life is to glorify God by doing his
> will and advancing his kingdom. This is crucial because when
> we were saved, the kingdom of God was set up in our hearts so
> that it might reach to and direct the circumference of our lives.
>   Having Jesus in your heart will get you to heaven. But
> having Jesus in your heart won't get heaven down into history.
> The Jesus in your heart must also be the Jesus who rules in the
> kingdom of which you are a part.[3]

We see this desire in the Lord's Prayer: "Your kingdom come, your will be done, on earth as it is in heaven" (Matt. 6:10). Christ prayed for us to live in God's kingdom, he died for us to live in God's kingdom, and he rose from the dead so we would live in God's kingdom. What does this mean for our call to mentoring? For starters, it means more good news! Not only did Christ pray, live, die, and rise for us to partake in his kingdom through the deposit of the Holy Spirit in the heart of every believer; Christ also *empowers us* to live for God's kingdom (Col. 2:9–10). God's kingdom is in and around us (Luke 17:21). It is ours to proclaim (Luke 9:60).

Those who mentor as intentional discipleship proclaim the good news of the kingdom of God. They understand the significance of their calling as the priesthood of God (1 Pet. 2:9) and as ambassadors for Christ (2 Cor. 5:18–20). They are deliberate, innovative, and creative in a world that is lost and dark. Together we glorify God because we are loving, creative, conscious, diverse, and beautiful. Raising up, releasing, and then multiplying followers of Christ to grow and flourish in *all* parts of the world and in *all* areas of life is purposeful and intentional kingdom work. As disciples and mentors of Christ, we are *all* delegated leaders in God's kingdom! Glory be to God!

Leadership in God's Kingdom

Through mentoring, we come to understand together that the kingdom of God in heaven is not like the kingdom of this world. God's kingdom is not built on the social, economic, or political power structures that define our typical relationships with others. His kingdom is not about hierarchy or who is in charge. It is not determined by titles, talents, or spiritual gifts. It isn't even based on whether we feel called to leadership.

To be clear, I believe *all* Christians are called to exercise spiritual authority as ambassadors of God on this earth. Yet because of our sinful hearts, we must be careful how we exercise that authority. God's authority is not given for the promotion of individual pursuits or to exert power over others—that is the way of Satan's kingdom.[4] God's authority is delegated to us. We are expected to be good stewards of our leadership. We should be humbled when we lead or serve others, recognizing that Christ is our ultimate authority and any influence we have is not about us—it is first about Christ and next about those he has called us to serve.

As Christians, we must ask, "Do we lead in the same manner as the rest of the world? Or do we follow the example of Jesus and lead by humbling ourselves as servants for the benefit of others?" People who are proud of their authority, titles, or spiritual gifts tend to lord it over those who may be less gifted in the ways they are, or they may be jealous of others who are gifted in ways they are not. On more than one occasion, Jesus chastised his disciples for their incorrect thinking concerning leadership in his kingdom (Luke 9:46–48 and Mark 10:35–44). To truly understand kingdom leadership, we look to Jesus who said of himself, "For even the Son of Man did not come to be served, but to serve, and to give his life as a ransom for many" (Mark 10:45).

The kingdom of God is about our freedom in Christ "You, my brothers and sisters, were called to be free. But do not use your freedom to indulge the flesh; rather, serve one another humbly in love" (Gal. 5:13). In God's kingdom, *all* Christians are graciously commissioned to pour out their lives in service for the priorities and purposes of God, and for the benefit of those God has called us to love. Through Christ, we have freely received salvation. Through the Holy Spirit, we have graciously been empowered. Be thankful, for mentoring at its best is done out of overflow from a grateful heart for these precious and unmerited gifts.

The Priesthood

Every kingdom has a rightful king. God is king, and as his children, "we are heirs—heirs of God and co-heirs with Christ" (Rom. 8:17). As heirs of God, we are reminded of our image-bearing identity and our kingdom-advancing responsibilities. Being a disciple of Christ means we have authority on this earth. God has not left us without hope in this world. He has given us the means to fight our Enemy and win! We do this by mentoring and equipping every Christian for spiritual warfare. Everyone must strengthen their arms, train for battle, and be willing to fight (Eph. 6:10–18; 2 Cor. 10:3–5). The mentoring principles shared in Part

II will prepare you and help you better understand how to train others to live a victorious life in the midst of these spiritual battles.

Like the faithful saints who have gone before us, we understand that this service of priesthood has been given to us as a gift[5] for a specific purpose. In his revelation, the apostle John honors Jesus as the one "who loves us and has freed us from our sins by his blood, and has made us to be a kingdom and priests to serve his God and Father—to him be glory and power for ever and ever!"[6] The priesthood includes *all* believers; we are all called to serve God and reveal his glory throughout the earth.

In the Old Testament, the priesthood was never simply about the individual priest's personal relationship and connection with God. The priests were always engaging God on behalf of God's chosen people. The priesthood is not only a personal positional privilege; it is also a great kingdom responsibility. I point this out because we often see many Christians fail to accept this responsibility. Several churches continue to operate under the Old Testament model of the priesthood where pastors and paid staff perform the work of the priesthood while other Christians sit around waiting for the church's leadership to tell them what to do. Certainly, we must honor our pastors, church staff, and spiritual influencers (Rom. 13:7). At the same time, we would do well to study the priesthood of all believers and take seriously the responsibility we *all* have to equip and prepare God's children for works of service. People are lost and dying; the spiritual battle is real, and as disciples of Christ, we need all followers on the front lines. The priests of God must prepare the people of God and set them free on mission for God's kingdom. *Christlike leaders and mentors liberate others and do not shackle them.* Paul affirmed this freedom for Christ followers when he wrote, "See to it that no one takes you captive through hollow and deceptive philosophy, which depends on human tradition and the elemental spiritual forces of this world rather than on Christ" (Col. 2:8).

A biblical understanding of the priesthood of all believers can empower us to embrace our responsibility to mentor. How? First, we empower others by raising their understanding of who they are and their expectations of what they can do. If laypeople are empowered to mentor, multiply, create, and live their lives on purpose for God, then we can moderate our expectations of pastors and their staffs. Embracing the priesthood of all believers means it is the responsibility of *all* Christians to intentionally live on purpose for God, while mentoring (discipling) others.

Understanding God's intention for us as his priests also changes the way we look at ourselves, each other, and our unique contributions to God's kingdom. As citizens in God's kingdom, we learn to "submit to one another out of reverence for Christ" (Eph. 5:21). We agree that the coming of Christ presents good news that has brought us all near to God (Eph. 2:13) and has empowered us to fulfill the purposes of his kingdom. We understand that God has equipped each of us with specific gifts, talents, and passions, which work together to glorify him and contribute to his kingdom. We hone these skills because with them, we cultivate the earth and infect it with God's glory. Andy Crouch writes:

> We can only create where we have learned to cultivate. . . . Cultivation is conservation—ensuring that the world we leave behind, whether natural or cultural, contains at least as many possibilities and at least as much excellence as the one we inherited. . . . The most demanding forms of cultivation are disciples—long apprenticeships in the rudiments of a cultural form, small things done over and over that create new capacities in us over time.[7]

You probably see by now why I love mentoring! In these early chapters, I am acknowledging up front that while it is rewarding, mentoring is also challenging and can sometimes be a disappointing experience. In those times, you will need to revisit these chapters and draw on the truth of God to motivate you and sustain your commitment to this important work. Although you might not see it on a daily basis, be assured that our actions are all a part of God's big master plan. I trust it gives you great encouragement and hope to know that we are on the winning side and that Christ is with us in all our struggles. It is with this truth and understanding that we prepare our hearts and minds for mentoring.

Let's do a quick summary of Part I: We mentor as intentional discipleship because making disciples is the crucial mission of the church. We mentor because mentoring establishes a connection between our traditional evangelistic practices and the call to make disciples. We mentor because mentoring shapes the church, and when done rightly, this in turn influences the broader culture.

Mentoring is the most effective way we equip children of God to live as honorable citizens in the world. As disciples, we stand against Satan because we are the possessors of God's kingdom (Matt. 16:17–20). We are privileged children, and our task as priests is monumental. We cannot entrust the work of the kingdom to a select few while the rest watch from the sidelines. As children of the King, we *all* share in the responsibility of mentoring and making disciples who make disciples.

The *good news* is that Christ has not left us defenseless or without hope in this spiritual war. He does not want us to grow weary or give up the fight. "His divine power has given us everything we need for a godly life through our knowledge of him who called us by his own glory and goodness" (2 Pet. 1:3). In Christ, we have the freedom to be exactly as God created us and to complete the work he has prepared in advance for us to do (Eph. 2:10). Through mentoring, we continually point people to Jesus and watch as the chains of Satan's kingdom are broken, and we are empowered to live victoriously as priests of God's kingdom! For this freedom, Christ has come (John 10:10).

But this work and commitment will not be easy. Daily, we

must submit ourselves to God and discipline ourselves to perse-vere. What we do consistently over extended periods of time will result in lasting change. As priests in God's kingdom, we have great responsibility:

> *When we see darkness, we make disciples who shine God's light.*
> *When we see evil, we make disciples who overcome evil with good.*
> *When we see oppression, we make disciples who practice biblical justice and offer hope.*
> *When we see the poor, we make disciples who invest time and give generously to liberate them.*
> *When we see hate, we make disciples who love.*
> *When we see risks, we make disciples who turn risks into opportunities.*
> *When we see children who are lost, we make disciples who mentor, tutor, and usher them into the presence of Christ.*
> *When we see doubters who say "No," we make disciples who say, "In Jesus' name, yes we can!"*

We must commit to the long haul, doing this work consistently until Christ returns, knowing that our Christian race is not given to the swift or strong but to those who endure until the end (Eccl. 9:11). We stand together as spiritual warriors, and we lock arms as a united priesthood to change the culture and transform the areas God has appointed for us to influence. We consider the cost of discipleship, remembering Jesus' words: "'No one who puts his hand to the plow and looks back is fit for service in the kingdom of God'" (Luke 9:62). As children of God, we shall not look back in admiration for the old, fallen kingdom and its lies. With the hope of our eternal salvation, the finished work of Christ on the cross, and the power of the Holy Spirit, we press forward to mentor and multiply.

Mentor for Life

1. How does the reality of spiritual warfare give perspective concerning the daily challenges and struggles you face as a Christian?

2. How has your awareness of being a part of God's priest-hood changed the way you view yourself and your responsibilities as a follower of Christ?

3. As you prepare your heart and mind for mentoring, what tools has God given you to watch, pray, and stand against the schemes of the Evil One?

4. What are your natural inclinations and responses to "weak links" in the body of Christ? As you prepare to mentor, how can you respond with both grace and truth to those at various stages of their faith journeys?

5. Summarize in four or five sentences what you have learned from this chapter.

Tweet This

"Mentoring at its best is done out of overflow from a grateful heart." #Mentor4Life @asistasjourney

Part Two

The Mentoring
Commitment

Principles and Practices

We've laid a foundation for mentoring by exploring the purpose and priorities, so let's shift our attention to focus on the commitment of mentoring, its principles, and its practices. This part of the book will answer the question, "How does mentoring take shape in the life of an individual believer?" We will discuss the discipline, training, and community cultivation necessary for healthy mentoring relationships to thrive. While practices of the mentoring commitment may look different depending on your community and church context, all Christians are called to a mentoring community of intentional discipleship.

The mentoring commitment is a commitment to relationships where disciples are equipped and encouraged to *know and love God, know who they are in Christ, and love their neighbors.* I will share the relational elements of mentoring—focusing first on our relationship with God, and then revealing how a proper relationship with God reflects in the God-honoring relationships we have with others.

A mentoring relationship must be approached humbly with the full understanding that the Holy Spirit is the one who works to change our hearts.[1] Human effort and skill alone will not bring lasting transformation. We should not take on that divine responsibility, but must surrender it to God. Through mentoring, we partner with God, agreeing with him that our hearts need change and surrendering to the means of change available through the power of the Holy Spirit. While the Holy Spirit works to change hearts, mentors can be used by God to facilitate the process of renewing a disciple's mind. A mentor teaches his or her disciples to put off their old selves and become new in the attitude of their minds by imitating God and walking in true righteousness and holiness.[2] As you read Part II, I encourage you to set your intentions on the following:

Christ

The goal of mentoring is to see hearts and minds transformed to reflect the image of Christ, to see relationships lovingly change, and to have disciples walk in their purpose to the glory of God. Christ is at the center of all our mentoring.[3] I pray that the commitment to mentoring will challenge you to grow in love and humility, and will continue to affirm your faith in Christ.

Community

When people think of mentoring, they often think of developing a one-on-one relationship with another person. Yet when we look at the Gospels, we see that Christ discipled within the context of a small group. If he is our Savior and Lord, then he must also be our primary mentor, and we are wise to follow his mentoring example. In cultivating mentoring relationships, mentors must not encourage an unhealthy dependency on themselves nor set unrealistic expectations for their mentees.

At the start of this commitment, you may need to help some women see that a one-on-one mentoring relationship is not what they most need. While there are certainly immeasurable benefits to one-on-one mentoring, those relationships tend to develop organically (possibly out of a mentoring small group). In this book, I focus on developing a healthy interdependency within a small mentoring community where women all focus on their true need for Christ and encourage one another to draw nearer to him.

Context

The remainder of the book develops a holistic approach for mentoring:

- Knowing and loving God
- Knowing your identity in Christ
- Loving your neighbor

These three pillars of mentoring reflect the Great Commandment given to us by Christ. This approach is theological (affirming what we know and believe) and ethical (accounting for what we actually practice), because both what we know *and* how we live matter in this world. To this end, I'll present six mentoring commitments: presence, discipline, mission, community, relationships, and love. At the conclusion of each mentoring commitment, I've included a "This Is How We Do It" summary so you can see what these principles look like in practice. It is important that you take the foundational principles provided in this book, evaluate your current ministry context, and then prayerfully discern how to incorporate them into your mentoring relationships.

Commitment

Spiritual growth is not a passive experience. The apostle Paul taught that Christians should train themselves to live godly lives. God calls us all to a spiritually disciplined life. Through the disciplines, he cultivates our hearts, strengthens our minds, and builds our stamina for a victorious faith journey. As we continue to grow, God will eventually make us confident enough to teach and train others.

A godly mentor will commit to sacrifice and lay down her life for the sake of others. Mentees will get out of mentoring what they are willing to put into the relationship—mentoring is a mutual commitment. Before you enter into a mentoring relationship with others, discuss the level of commitment, set expectations and boundaries, and decide on a method of accountability and correction. Having this conversation early and often will ensure a safe and trusting mentoring community that is a healthy environment for learning and relationship building.

Let us prepare our hearts and minds for this commitment, shall we?

Mentoring

A Commitment to Presence

*Somehow we have come to believe that good
leadership requires a safe distance from those we are
called to lead. . . . Someone serves, someone else is
being served, and be sure not to mix up the roles!
But how can anyone lay down his life for those with
whom he is not even allowed to enter into a deep
personal relationship? Laying down your life means
making your own faith and doubt, hope and despair,
joy and sadness, courage and fear available to others
as a way of getting in touch with the Lord of life.*

Henri J. M. Nouwen[1]

Being present with God and present in community with
other disciples is essential for our spiritual transformation.

Mentoring as intentional discipleship reminds us of our desperate
need for God's presence and the community of God's
people, which we miss when our lives are consumed with
noise and distractions.

Five

Presence with God

I believe silence is the most challenging, the most needed and the least experienced spiritual discipline among evangelical Christians today.

Ruth Haley Barton[1]

Let's face it—women are busy. Yet there is a difference between being busy and being productive. As productive citizens of God's kingdom, I believe all God's daughters can live full and intentional lives as we draw near to the One we love, and to the One we know loves us. Productive women live their lives on purpose, with intentionality, and they serve and sacrifice for the sake of the call, the giftedness, and the work God has uniquely outlined for them. We are all born with a purpose. Part of fulfilling that purpose is learning to lay down the things that keep us busy but distracted from the important work of God's kingdom and learning to pursue with passion and focus the things God has assigned to each of us. Mentoring starts with the acknowledgment of God's presence and the understanding of how God's presence shapes our relationships with others.

Focusing on God's kingdom mission helps us prioritize mentoring relationships over the many things that can keep us busy and distracted. Women won't commit to mentoring others for various reasons. Some women believe they just don't have the time to mentor well. Some older women feel they are not equipped to

mentor or they incorrectly conclude that they don't have much
to offer. Younger women may be juggling careers, school, and
relationships. They may want mentoring but don't know whom
to ask or how to get started. Most people simply don't want to add
one more thing to their already overflowing plates, and mentoring
seems like a huge undertaking. But there is good news! Mentoring
is not the burden you might expect. It's more than just another
thing to add to your full list of tasks. Mentoring is a gift from
God, an opportunity to experience his presence as you join on
his mission in community with others. We must stop seeing mentoring and making disciples as a burdensome task and reclaim it
as the blessing, responsibility, and privilege it is. Discipling others
gives us the opportunity to respond in obedience to God. In this
obedience, there is great joy.

Reevaluating Our Needs

If we have already set our own agendas and have predetermined
what we will do with our lives, we will not yield to the kingship
of God. Jesus alone knows us by name; he alone knows what we
need before we ask him (Matt. 6:8), and he alone can meet that
need. Before we discuss anything else, we must accept this as true.
We need to see that Jesus is ultimately the one who meets our
needs, not the one mentoring or the one being mentored. In one-
on-one mentoring relationships, there is potential for unhealthy
codependency between the mentor and mentee because one or
both parties enter with unrealistic expectations. But the goal of
the mentoring commitment is to help each other recognize our
desperate need for God so we learn to depend on him. This is why
a mentor's first responsibility is to cultivate her own relationship
with the Lord.

The first pillar of the mentoring ministry is knowing and loving God. The truth is, all God is asking from any of us is that we

show up to meet with him. He calls us to seek first his kingdom, and he promises to shower us with good things and to give us rest for our weary souls.

Drawing Nearer to God

To practice the discipline of "showing up," take a few moments to complete this short exercise:

Pause now in a quiet place that does not have any distractions. Take a few minutes of silence, and breathe deeply. As you inhale and exhale, allow your mind to relax. Don't think about anything other than what you are doing right now. Now, reflect on the following passages of God's Word for you today:

It is better to take refuge in the LORD *than to trust in humans.* (Ps. 118:8)

"Come to me, all you who are weary and burdened, and I will give you rest." (Matt. 11:28)

But as for me, it is good to be near God. I have made the Sovereign LORD *my refuge; I will tell of all your deeds.* (Ps. 73:28)

Sometimes we need to meditate on the truth of God's Word and repeat it to ourselves so it presses deeply into our hearts and minds: *As for me, it is good to be near God. As for me, it is good to be near God. It is good to be near God.* Listen to your heart. Do you long to be near God? Do you intentionally seek his presence? Presence is often missing from our busy lives.

Presence means *being fully engaged right where we are.* Sometimes we miss the intimate moments of our lives because we are distracted, trying to capture them with a camera or document them through social media. Have you ever been to a school play or a family sports outing only to notice that half of the adults are watching the event through their smartphones? While there is value in saving memories for later, this habit means we often miss being present in the moment. Sometimes we are not present because we are trying to play God—we move too fast and try to accomplish too much without acknowledging the limitations of our humanity and the constraints of our time. We have conditioned ourselves for these distractions, so when we have an opportunity to sit in silence before God or be fully present with others, we are uncomfortable. When our fragile hearts find comfort in noise, we know we are living in the false security of distraction.

Noise prevents us from clearly hearing the voice of God when he speaks. However, we need the stillness of the present moment to intentionally meet with God. Being present takes us away from the noise and draws us into a place of solitude and silence. "Solitude is not a private therapeutic place. Rather, it is the *place of conversion*, the place where the old self dies and the new self is born, the place where the emergence of the new man and the new woman occurs."[2] Think about it: what prayers we could utter, what problems we could solve, what things we would remember if we simply started spending a little time in silence every day in order to be present with God.

We may shun silence because it can be a fearful place, but when we commit to embrace silence, we also take a stand against the noise that carries all the world's messages, the distractions of life, and the pressing in of our culture.

God's Presence and Making Connections

We lack vision and inspiration about the good we can create if we are constantly condemning, critiquing, copying, and consuming cultural noise.[3] If we are not intentional about being present with God, we run the risk of subconsciously internalizing the false messages of the world and we become distracted from living our lives on purpose. Committing to a mentoring community helps us intentionally show up to meet with God and reject the lies of the

world. Being present in accountable, reflective, and transformative mentoring relationships reminds us of God's truth and of our
identity in Christ. We are less likely to casually fall into the danger
of believing in a false sense of identity. It is a sign of immatu-
rity when we would rather settle into the comfort we know than
confront the discomfort we don't understand. The result of idly
accepting the world's lies and a false identity, and of living with
unconfessed sin, leads us to incorrectly believe we are not that bad
off, God doesn't care, and maybe we don't need him at all. The
truth is, we *do* need God.

When I was a seminary student, I attended chapel service
every Friday evening. We gathered around 6:00 p.m., and the
lights were dimly lit. Oftentimes, there were moments of silence.
Some students had their Bibles open. Others were in deep thought.
Some simply sat alone, decompressing from a long week of full-
time work and ministry, family commitments, and studies. We
all came together in that place spiritually needy and desperate for
God. By 6:30, the first string of the guitar was plucked and we
were singing words to one of my favorite hymns: *Come thou fount
of every blessing, tune my heart to sing thy grace* . . . By the time we
reached the third stanza, arms were lifted as hearts were raised
up and laid bare before our blessed King. Tears rolled down our
cheeks. We had met with Jesus. We were present.

> *Prone to wander, Lord, I feel it,*
> *Prone to leave the God I love;*
> *Here's my heart, O take and seal it,*
> *Seal it for thy courts above.*

We are all prone to wander and leave our precious Savior. After
the apostle Peter denied Jesus three times, he knew he could not
trust his own heart. Jesus, in his mercy, sent the other disciples after
him, and he was restored into community. The apostle Paul, James,
and the writer of Hebrews all came to understand this tendency

to wander as well, and that's why they wrote so passionately about perseverance, steadying the spiritual course, and running our spiritual race together. In my own life, I, too, have come to understand the struggle against accepting a false sense of identity and the temptation to stray from intimate fellowship with the Lord. This is why I need others in my life to mentor, guide, and correct me. Living as a disciple of Christ means we fellowship with others and regularly die to our false selves, so that Christ can continuously resurrect us as new people who are perfected in his image.

Do you struggle to consistently show up in your relationships with other people? Are you absent physically, emotionally, intellectually, or spiritually? Our failure to show up for others may be rooted in a lack of desire and discipline to show up and be present with God. The desire for God's presence is an expression of our hearts' condition before him, but it is also a humble acknowledgment of our need for strength, wisdom, discernment, courage, guidance, and the help only he can provide. When we engage in mentoring others and submit to being mentored by them, we understand that we all have these same needs, and that no one follower of Christ is an island, self-sufficient apart from the rest of the body.

Roena moved to town a few years ago. She is in her forties, a married stay-at-home mom who always has a smile on her face. When she joined our church, Roena jumped right in and started serving. I thought to myself, "This is someone who understands God's kingdom mission. She is a sure candidate for leadership in the mentoring ministry." But before we could go there, we had to address her felt need. You see, being new, Roena did not have many friends. Over a little food, chocolate, and fellowship in my home, Roena quickly became connected with several other women. She joined a mentoring group where her mentor acknowledged Roena's spiritual maturity and the contributions she was making to the group. I also continued to engage Roena in informal conversations throughout the year, and came to know her as a woman of great depth, someone who was acquainted with suffering and had a heart for broken women.

After a year of observation, we asked Roena to prayerfully consider joining the mentoring ministry leadership team. Roena was unsure about mentoring and knew she had a lot to learn, but we believed our hearts and hers would be shaped and changed by her presence on the leadership team.

During training, I taught Roena and others the importance of knowing and loving God and being in his presence. In addition to disciplines like Bible reading and Scripture memorization, we completed exercises that helped us enter into the Lord's presence. One exercise in particular, the "Letter from God,"[4] was inspired by God's letter to the seven churches in Revelation 2–3. The exercise was a personal reflection on our current spiritual condition before God. It acknowledged where the mentor or mentee was hearing God's affirmation, where she was hearing a gentle rebuke or challenge from God, and identified the possible consequences of disobedience or possible rewards and blessings for obedience. All our mentors and mentees went through this exercise in their private moments of silence with God before sharing their personal letters with their mentoring groups.

Roena let me know that she felt this particular exercise was especially difficult for her to complete. She confessed she was not ready to hear what God was going to speak to her. She was afraid to pour out her heart before him. She knew she needed to ask for forgiveness for holding on to things too tightly and for not giving him complete control over her life. Yet she took the risk, completed the assignment, and found that God was indeed present with her. Here is what she wrote:

Dear Roena,

I know your deeds, that you are mentoring a group at church. I know you are also participating in another in-depth Bible study so you can further grow in my Word. I see you surrendering your daily plans to encourage others with acts of service. These are all good things, but this one thing I hold against you: you are trying to do these in your own strength and are not relying on me to sustain you. You are complaining that you cannot lead a mentoring group because you do not know enough about the Bible, because you are too young, because you have never taught before, and because you do not have all the answers to the mentees' questions. You are overwhelmed with all the reading and preparation. You complain but do not come to me, your Sustainer, who wants to give you help.

Because I love you, I will not allow you to stay comfortable in your faith. I am stretching you to the point where you have no other choice but to give everything to me and trust me in the areas where you are weak. If you fail to surrender control, you will not grow like I have planned, and you will miss opportunities that I have for you to minister in my Name. But if you submit and obey my lead, then you will live a blessed life with fulfillment you can receive only through me. You will bring honor to me and find happiness in me alone. Press on, my child. Forget about yourself, and keep your eyes on me. I promise never to leave or forsake you.

I love you,
Abba God

God met Roena in this place of silence and vulnerability with an affirming message of truth and love. He gave her the encouragement, support, and gentle correction she needed within the context of our leadership team. Presence with God and being present in community with others is essential for our spiritual formation. When we truly draw near to God, we find ourselves drawing near to other people as well.

The opposite is also true. If we subconsciously buy into the lie that we do not need God, then we will also regularly buy into the lie that we don't need other people. Although he was the perfect God-man, Jesus took time to pray in his Father's presence.[5] He also took his friends along to pray during his most vulnerable moment.[6] Just as Jesus modeled for us, presence with God increases our openness with and vulnerability before others, especially during times of pain and suffering. We model the life of our Savior when we seek the Father's presence and commit to being present in community.

God's presence is what we most desperately need. When we are in his presence, he leads us. In a mentoring community, we participate with God and make ourselves available to the work of the Holy Spirit, which sanctifies the hearts of individuals. Mentors surrender by first drawing near to God themselves. Then by example, they teach and model for their mentees how to enter into the presence of God. Being present is our hearts' true longing, and when that longing is satisfied, it fills the voids in our lives and draws us closer to others. God is the daily bread we so desperately need. Reject the lies. Shut out the noise. Cease striving. Come thirsty. Find your purpose in the presence of God.

Mentor for Life

1. In what ways do you tend to be distracted by the noise of life?

2. How do you intentionally pursue God's presence (intimate relationship or spending time with the Lord)?

3. As a mentor, what are some intentional ways you can encourage mentees to embrace the gifts of silence, solitude, and presence with God?

4. As a mentor, what ways can you welcome the gift of silence even in your mentoring community? Consider the differences between engaging those who are introverted and extroverted with an attitude of mutual submission, shared participation, and value in a mentoring group.

5. Presence Exercise: Use the example provided in this chapter to complete the "Letter from God" exercise. How do you believe God sees you?

6. Summarize in four or five sentences what you have learned from this chapter.

Tweet This

Presence: "All God is asking from any of us is that we show up to meet with him." #Mentor4Life @asistasjourney

Six

Presence with Others

> To cultivate a growthful and open mentoring process,
> foster intrigue about people's behavior—both successes and
> failures—and excitement about the process of discovery that
> leads to clarity.
>
> *Robert J. Wicks[1]*

If you truly desire to know and love God, to understand your identity in Christ Jesus, and to love your neighbor as yourself, you must confront the reality that in our own capacity, the ability to live authentically is beyond reach. Henri J. M. Nouwen writes, "Anyone who wants to fight his demons with his own weapons is a fool. The . . . confrontation with our own frightening nothingness forces us to surrender ourselves totally and unconditionally to the Lord Jesus Christ."[2] Total surrender is the call of a disciplined life. Like solitude, surrender is a scary process—particularly for Americans who are under the false assumption that we are in control. God calls us, as disciples, to release the illusion of control and enter into his presence.

In the silence of God's presence, we can acknowledge our personal struggles and confess that we have grown comfortable in our sinful, self-destructive habits. In this sacred place, we exchange our false sense of identity and come to embrace the person God wants us to be, though that person is a stranger to us. Early in my Christian walk, I got excited while reading Romans 8:28: "And we know that in all things God works for the good of those who love him, who have been called according to his purpose." As a new believer, I thought, "Wow! I love the Lord, and I'm called according to his purpose, so he is going to work things out for my good." Shortly after that, I faced heartache, struggle, and disappointment.

During those years of suffering, God opened my eyes to embrace what he is really saying in this passage. Verse 29 continues, "For those God foreknew he also predestined to be conformed to the image of his Son." I had read that passage countless times before finally making the connection that God's good for me is to transform me into the image of his Son, Jesus. God promises to use every good thing in my life as well as every heartbreak, difficulty, and struggle toward this end. *Coming to Jesus is not a call to a struggle-free life. It is a call to follow him through our life's struggles because we are completely surrendered to God.*

Never Alone

Melva stopped by my lunch table at the restaurant to introduce herself. We were members of the same church, and upon learning that I was launching a new women's mentoring ministry, she shared with me her own passion for mentoring and her desire to lead a mentoring group. We had just completed our leadership training for the year, but I encouraged her to connect in a mentoring group and agreed to let her know when we would provide leadership training for the following mentoring season.

I soon learned that Melva was a caretaker for her husband, and in addition to managing his care and serving faithfully in the church, she had a full-time job working outside of the home. Melva was suffering, but her life had been greatly impacted by a mentor in her younger years. Her heart was naturally drawn to the mentoring ministry, and in spite of her other commitments, she still had the desire to lead a mentoring group. Given all her responsibilities, it seemed unlikely that she would be able to commit to leadership the following year.

Then Melva wrote to me:

> In April 2012, my husband affirmed his opinion that I should lead a mentoring group: "You need to do it. I'm going to be fine." In spite of my husband being placed in hospice care later that month, God began to give me peace about making this commitment to mentor. Then Willie went home to be with the Lord. He was finally free of pain. It was bittersweet. As the numbness and exhaustion of grief set in, I clung to God and the women in my mentoring group who graciously and lovingly cared for me during this difficult time. Through prayer, fellowship, and the mentoring ministry, God began to strengthen me and show me His sovereignty. He reminded me that His timing is perfect and in my moments of weakness, He is strong. I lived this reality with confidence that one of my husband's last wishes was for me to serve the Lord by mentoring women.
>
> Three months later, a mentoring group began to meet in my home. My home, which previously posed a logistical challenge for mentoring because of the coming and going of aides and caregivers, now became a place of silence—a perfect place for a mentoring group to gather. God knew that I first needed the support of a mentoring group during a very difficult time in my life, and now I can share with other women that no matter your circumstance or suffering, you are not alone.

Through the presence of others in community, God reminds us that we are never alone. He uses every relationship, every heartache and suffering, to transform us and remind us that he is near. We will not experience the blessings of this loving support and care if we do not have authentic relationships and community. Oftentimes, people desire the blessings of community but are unwilling to commit to cultivating relationships.

Committing to a Mentoring Community

Melva's decision to submit in a mentoring community for a year before taking on a leadership role as a mentor communicated a lot about her spiritual maturity and her motivations. This is an important case study for mentors because we must understand that the mentoring community is not only shaped by what we do; the mentoring community will also reflect the passions and intentions of all—both mentor and mentees—involved. The mentees' attitude will determine whether spiritual formation actually takes place in the mentoring group. Mentees must be willing to learn and to commit to the process of spiritual formation.

I recall one of my former mentors who lived in another state asking for my advice regarding some challenges she was having with a mentee who was close to my age, a young woman I'd never met. My mentor was concerned about several negative habits she was observing and was afraid she might not be able to successfully encourage the young woman to make better choices. As I listened, I began to recognize several of those same characteristics in myself—so I blurted out, "I'm like that, too!" And it was true! Without skipping a beat, my friend and mentor responded, "But you're teachable." Reflecting on this confession of my heart, I understand that maturity and the perseverance of faith is not about one's condition when beginning the faith journey, but it does consider whether or not we will submit to God, heed wise counsel, and have a teachable spirit.

The reality is that we are all flawed people in desperate need of God's grace. As we mentor and are mentored by others, our flaws will be exposed. We can receive God's grace through the help, encouragement, and support of others, but spiritual transformation will happen only if we are present in relationship with others. This is why submitting to mentoring relationships is so important.

Saved or unsaved, all flawed people need to hear the truth of God spoken in love. Yet the relationship alone is not enough. We must be open to change. We must be teachable.

A mentoring community can lovingly support us by offering accountability and gentle correction, and by praying that we cultivate a teachable heart. Spending time in the presence of others who have traveled down a certain road can help us learn from their mistakes and avoid making mistakes of our own. The sad truth, however, is that not everyone heeds wise counsel. Therefore, a potential mentee must be challenged concerning her intentions. Her decision to be mentored must include a willing investment in her spiritual growth and a desire to love and be present with God and others. Mentees must prepare. Mentees must show up.

Presence and preparation lead to growth and change. Mentors invest in women who invest in themselves. This personal investment for both mentor and mentee is really a decision of surrender. Having a teachable, submissive, and humble spirit means laying all of ourselves and our baggage before God and allowing him lordship over every area of our lives. We cannot serve our own agendas and surrender to the Lord at that same time.

Sadly, not every woman in your church, friendship circle, workplace, or neighborhood will want to sacrifice or surrender their lives to God. When considering a relationship with a new mentee, you are not looking for her to have everything together. On the contrary. You are simply looking for the woman who is open and willing to change. Pray for God to send along women who have teachable spirits.

As you begin your mentoring relationships, encourage mentees to share their faith journey with those in the group (some may not have much to share, and that's okay). You can share your own faith journey, the hope you have in the Lord, and help them see that the Lord is at work in the world. Give them freedom to dream about where the Lord might be leading. Allow your initial encounters and group gathering to shape your expectations and the culture you develop within the mentoring group. Encourage and challenge them along the way. Don't compromise the cross-bearing elements of spiritual formation in an attempt to draw more mentees. I am a witness that we have seen great spiritual transformation by mentors and mentees only when they are committed to the mentoring community and only when they are open to growth and change.

A Look in the Mirror

Change can be scary. Embracing spiritual transformation requires that we come face-to-face with God and face-to-face with ourselves. Sometimes I am initially saddened or frightened by what is revealed about myself during my alone time with God; however, in his presence I have come to better understand Nouwen's words:

> Only in the context of grace can we face our sin; only in the place of healing do we dare to show our wounds; only with a single-minded attention to Christ can we give up our clinging fears and face our own true nature. As we come to realize that it is not we who live, but Christ who lives in us, that he is our true self, we can slowly let our compulsions melt away and begin to experience the freedom of the children of God.[3]

In his presence, we do receive grace. In his presence, he clarifies our purpose, and we are reminded that we are free to simply *be*.

Being is something we cultivate in community. After creating man, God looked at his good creation and said, "It is *not* good for the man to be alone" (Gen. 2:18, emphasis mine). God made this statement even though man was created sinless, and despite the fact that man was fully enjoying intimacy in God's presence. Because he did not want man to dwell alone, God made a companion for Adam who was like himself[a] and only then did God declare his creation "very good" (Gen. 1:31). From the beginning, we were meant to understand that human beings need each other.

Carmen is a stay-at-home, homeschooling mom of four boys, and a devoted follower of Christ. She has experienced transformation in her own life through the daily surrender and sacrifice of being in a committed mentoring community:

> It's 4:00 p.m. Dirty dishes line the sink. School books are on the floor. Children are noisy and playing. Some are crying, others are fighting. In my mind, I consider my daily duties and know that this is not how a heart gets prepared to mentor. But this is my life, and God has called me to mentor. Every month is the same. I question every time if this is what I should be doing. I wrangle children at the last minute, spill my words, and frantically run around the house, which always seems a mess. We rush to finish the kids' homework, and I am praying all the while that God would empty me of myself so I can pour out to him. I know this is not how you prepare to serve, minister, or encourage others. When I said "yes" to mentoring, I must have forgotten what filled our 4:00 hour! But every month, the hour looks the same. This is what my heart looks like, and many times I've just wanted to cancel the mentoring gathering because I seemed unprepared, distracted, or conflicted.
>
> My family would normally depart for dinner and an outing while the women settled in our home for mentoring. When the clock hits 5:00 p.m., the Lord reminds me that obedience is better than sacrifice. This reminder encourages me to continue the work of mentoring. When the women come, God uses a frazzled mom to speak truth. God uses a worn and weary wife to pray for the needs of his precious daughters. God uses my living room—a room that only moments ago was filled with disunity and misunderstanding—to create unity and understanding among the hearts of women. Every time, our hours together are filled with praise, prayer, and

partnering. With all the work, worry, and whining, the sacrifice seemed too great at 4:00, but for me, God has used each night of mentoring to see his hand at work. In the presence of these women, I am reminded that sacrifice is not always what I have to give, but what I might miss when I am not willing to give up.

Carmen's testimony reminds us that God meets us in our moments of self-sacrifice and surrender, and He extends grace sufficient for our need. More than anything—more than prep time, a nap, a clean house—his presence is what we really need. Through mentoring, he has given us the gift of practicing presence and *being* with him and in community with others, which is essential for our spiritual formation.

This Is How We Do It

So what does cultivating a mentoring community that is present with God and present with others look like? First, we ask the women in the mentoring groups to commit to showing up. The mentoring season consists of ten group gatherings per year, for a gathering time of three hours each.[5] Every mentor and mentee makes a one-year commitment (ten months active participation, two months of Sabbath rest which may include an informal fellowship or retreat). Since they are meeting only monthly and are setting their own mentoring schedule, the expectation is for everybody to attend every monthly gathering.[6]

We ask that they bring all of themselves to the table or to the couch. We ask that they are present. We ask that they turn off their cell phones and pay no attention to their watches. We remind them that community is intentionally developed. Building community and cultivating real relationships is an investment. It takes work.

We grow in community when each of us shows up prepared to listen attentively, to ask questions, and to observe what is being communicated or not communicated. Community investments also include the time each of us spends alone with God completing our mentoring exercises between group gathering times. Presence requires that we adequately prepare and commit to learn from each other. None of us have all the answers, and this frees us to simply love, seek truth, and learn in mutual submission. Through mentoring, we are alert to listen with our eyes, ears, and hearts. We also acknowledge that God alone will nurture us individually through spiritual disciplines, as he nourishes us collectively in community.

To help mentees learn the three mentoring pillars of *knowing and loving God, knowing your identity in Christ Jesus, and loving your neighbor,* we read three books together as a group. These books are intentionally selected by the leadership team to encourage theological reflection, disciple our minds through the study of God's Word, and help us develop a Christian worldview, all the while cultivating deeper relationships with each other. Our commitment to this process of learning reveals that we have a teachable spirit and a desire for spiritual formation.

In addition to the reading, mentors and mentees often set aside time as part of their mentoring curriculum to memorize Scripture, answer personal reflection questions, and complete exercises that accompany their reading or journaling. These reinforcing corrective elements occur in a *place of conversion.* The place of conversion is not a physical location, but rather a term used by Henri Nouwen to communicate that time and space has been set aside to intentionally commune with God and be in his presence. It is more than a quiet time or devotion, as our modern-day understanding of those terms tend to communicate very short time commitments and very little depth. The place of conversion is where our relationship with God is nurtured. Nouwen describes the place of conversion as "the place where the old self dies and the new self is born, the place where the emergence of the new man and the new woman occurs."[7] It is the place of transformation. This transformation occurs in the mentoring group gathering, during the times mentors and mentees set aside to work through their mentoring curriculum, and as they cultivate the spiritual disciplines.

The place of conversion gives women an opportunity to intentionally reflect on and discuss the mentoring resources they have read. They accomplish the former by completing an exercise we refer to as a book net-out[8]—a one page (either handwritten or typed) personal reflective summary that includes identified key themes from the reading, their personal "takeaways," and a specific practical application. They accomplish the latter by sharing their book net-outs with their mentoring group. The purpose of all mentoring exercises is to increase the mentee's understanding and enhance her intimate moments spent alone with God and in fellowship with her mentoring community.

Being in a mentoring community has proven that the discipline of studying together greatly contributes to our understanding of God and ourselves. A. W. Tozer writes, "What comes to our minds when we think about God is the most important thing about us."[9] Since study increases our knowledge of God and self, we must learn to discipline ourselves to study. In his classic book, *Celebration of Discipline*, Richard J. Foster outlines four steps of study: repetition, concentration, comprehension, and reflection, while recognizing that humility is also needed.[10] Appendix A denotes how we incorporate all of these steps of study into our mentoring ministry, which allows us to enter the place of conversion both individually and collectively.

One of the resources we used for *knowing and loving God* during the first year of mentoring was A. W. Tozer's *The Pursuit of God*. This classic is a short but challenging read. Many of the women had never read anything at this level of difficulty. As I engaged several mentees for feedback throughout the mentoring season, one of the mentees shared her routine for approaching Tozer: "I sit down with that book, my Bible, and a dictionary, and then I pray for the Holy Spirit to help me understand." That's a woman who is intentional about entering the Lord's presence; that's a woman who is concentrating and preparing to study! I vividly recall another mentee texting me in the middle of the night because she was starting to understand and embrace the message of pursuing God. She could hardly contain herself! This reading, these exercises, and unique mentoring opportunities excited women by challenging them to renew their minds and change the way they think!

You must know, there will be some women who are not teachable, who are not interested in learning or cultivating their relationship with the Lord. But there will always be women who want to spend time alone with God and who want deeper relationships with other women. Those women need your help. This is the sacred offering of presence available through mentoring.

Mentor for Life

1. Do you have a teachable spirit? How well do you respond to correction, constructive criticism, or a gentle rebuke? How might you cultivate a teachable spirit? Can you think of someone who would be willing to help you?

2. What comes to mind when you think about God?

3. What might God be asking you to give up, sacrifice, or surrender to actively participate in a mentoring community with others?

4. Are you afraid to mentor? How might you overcome your uncertainties and fears and take the risk of mentoring others?

5. Presence Exercise: Set a lunch or coffee date with a small group (three or four) of trusted friends. Inform them of your desire to have a focused conversation about your responses to the questions in this chapter. Ask them to carefully consider your concerns and offer helpful feedback.

6. Summarize in four or five sentences what you have learned from this chapter.

Tweet This

"God's presence is not something that we only pursue in isolation; it also requires community."
#Mentor4Life @asistasjourney

Mentoring

A Commitment to a Disciplined Life

Engaging in spiritual practices is not a formula for transformation but rather the ongoing experience of "the Mystery of God in its breadth and depth." Indeed, there is mystery in our relationship with God, and the human mind may objectify this mystery through rote or mechanized behavior . . . When motivated by a pure heart (Matt. 5:8) to commune with God . . . spiritual practices become doorways for the Spirit to work deeply in the human heart, drawing us further into worship by way of a reciprocal love relationship.

Diane J. Chandler[1]

Spiritual disciples help us recognize our spiritual poverty and desperate need for God.

Mentoring as intentional discipleship incorporates spiritual disciplines to encourage us to right thinking and right action.

Seven

Discipleship of the Mind

*The theme of knowing and doing—what Os Guinness calls the
responsibility of knowledge—is central to the Christian faith.*
James W. Sire[1]

Spiritual disciplines can provide daily nourishment for a hungry
soul. For thousands of years, they have shaped the hearts of people
of faith. When approached with the right motivation, they can be
the catalysts that take us into the very presence of God and gives us
focus to serve the people and purposes of God. Spiritual disciplines
are not practices of a new covenantal law; they are not meant to be
burdensome. They are a means of God's grace meant to set us free
from our own bondage and self-absorption. Spiritual disciplines
invite us into the Lord's presence to embrace our true selves so we
can live authentically and love others well. They are a means of
discipline for our minds and for our souls.

The intent of the "Commitment to a Disciplined Life" section
is not to present an exhaustive overview of the spiritual disciplines.
Instead, I want us to explore the purpose of the spiritual disciplines
with a particular emphasis on those we can cultivate and practice
through mentoring relationships.

In the previous section, I mentioned the spiritual disciplines
of solitude and silence. These highlight our need for undistracted

time alone with God and focused time with others. In this section, we will discover additional disciplines to consider for mentoring, and I'll explain how to create a *place of conversion* where you and your mentees can meet with God.

One of the overlooked disciplines of the Christian faith, especially among laypeople, is God's command that we love the Lord with our minds. When asked about the greatest commandment, Jesus replied, "Love the Lord your God with all your heart and with all your soul and *with all your mind*."[2] When I'm training new mentors, one of the key Scriptures I regularly reference is Romans 12:2: "Do not conform to the pattern of this world, but *be transformed by the renewing of your mind*. Then you will be able to test and approve what God's will is—his good, pleasing and perfect will" (emphasis added). This chapter focuses on the discipleship or renewal of our minds. When I mention discipleship in this context, I am referring to the importance of training our minds to think rightly, or rather to focus on the proper things.

As a young child, the importance of knowledge, education, and becoming a lifelong learner was all around me. I remember slogans like, "Knowledge Is Power" and "A Mind Is a Terrible Thing to Waste."[3] Through these messages, I understood that knowledge is not gained for its own sake, and the mind is not brilliant for our own benefit. Knowledge exposes us to new information and releases us to engage that information. When our minds are unlocked, we gain courage to go places and do things we never dreamed of before. As a high school freshman, I recall passionately singing, "If you wanna be somebody and you wanna go somewhere, you better wake up and pay attention."[4] My identity in Christ affirms that I am somebody! I know the power of the Holy Spirit works to ensure God's redemptive purposes are carried out in this world, and it is God's desire to accomplish that work through people like you and me. It is with this understanding that we must wake up and pay attention!

Encouraging God's people to get their minds right and pay attention to what's going on in the world is part of our mentoring commitment. We have a charge to consider how God wants us to live and respond. The call to a disciplined life includes discipline of both the mind and the soul, for when they are engaged, we learn to respond rightly. Transformation begins in the mind. Right thinking produces right actions. We also learned from the previous chapter that right actions can produce right thinking. (Consistently showing up and committing to a mentoring group is a right action that can lead to transformation.) Through mentoring, we make this connection and commit to both right thinking and right actions.

Allow me to show you an example of how this works through my own pursuit of biblical justice. While I am clear that we will not all be convicted or passionate about the same issues of injustice, I share this journey in particular because I believe the pursuit of biblical justice is sometimes a neglected aspect of our discipleship. This apathy and neglect is often a result of the lack of proper training and teaching in this regard.[5]

From Right Thinking to Right Action

Several years ago, I went through an in-depth study on the topic of biblical justice with a mentor. As a mentor myself, I carried, and still carry, the responsibility to share the wisdom and knowledge I receive with others. As a student of the Bible, I understand that teaching and training mentors about an unfamiliar topic like biblical justice requires that I use our mentoring framework to approach the idea of justice theologically with the Word of God. Our mentoring framework includes *loving our neighbors*. Love compels us to renew our minds in relation to the way we think about people, which determines how we respond to them. Pastor Eddie Byun writes:

The most basic meaning [of justice] is "to treat people well," but it also carries the meaning of giving people what is due them, be it protection or punishment. And the word for justice in the Greek is *dikaiosyne*, which is most commonly translated as "righteousness." It is right living in the context of community.[6]

We mentors learn to love well by first renewing our minds so we can respond rightly to the injustices in our communities. At the heart of this renewal is the theological question, "How does pursuing justice make us better lovers of our neighbors?" Getting our minds wrapped around a right response to that question is the catalyst to responding with the right actions. During my study of biblical justice, I organized an anti-human trafficking education and awareness series in our community. I asked one of my friends for her assistance.

Jennifer is a social worker by profession. We were asking similar questions about justice. Through her social work, Jennifer knew about human trafficking, but she had not done anything with that knowledge. During her third season of mentoring, however, her reading included Timothy Keller's *Generous Justice: How God's Grace Makes Us Just* and Mark Labberton's *The Dangerous Act of Loving Your Neighbor*. Because she was renewing her mind in a mentoring group and wrestling with her desire to love others well, I didn't have to convince her to take a stand against human trafficking in our local community. Renewing her mind had a profound impact on her identity and her sense of calling. She shares:

> I was privileged to read these books that I might not have picked up on my own. They presented the biblical concept of seeking justice for the oppressed and loving others by truly seeing them through the eyes of Jesus. Driven to my Bible again and again, I studied these topics and began to understand why and how God wanted me to personally seek justice for the oppressed, and I realized my passion for becoming an advocate

for victims of human trafficking. When given the opportunity to serve in the human trafficking education and awareness series, I no longer thought of it as a good project. Taking action was a way of loving others and part of God's calling on my life.

Renewing our minds is a matter of training ourselves to think as God thinks. When we do so, we find that God's grace transforms who we are and he makes us more like him. Through mentoring, we surrender to him and discipline ourselves to read intentionally and become lifelong learners because right thinking produces right actions.

Renewing the Mind in Love and War

In an earlier chapter, we learned that spiritual warfare is waging in the world. If we pay attention, we notice when it is physically manifested, as in the sin of human trafficking. At other times, however, the attacks of the Enemy are more subtle, and if we are not watchful, we become victims of them. Such spiritual attacks on our minds include the acceptance of lies and messages received from the culture and the world. Second Corinthians 10:3–5 speaks about how spiritual battles are fought in our minds:

> For though we live in the world, we do not wage war as the world does. The weapons we fight with are not the weapons of the world. On the contrary, they have divine power to demolish strongholds. We demolish arguments and every pretension that sets itself up against the knowledge of God, and *we take captive every thought to make it obedient to Christ.* (Emphasis mine.)

There is no doubt about it—as Christians, we must discipline our minds, and we must take captive every thought to make it obedient to Christ. It is a matter of life and death.

Because we understand the significance of renewing our minds and training them for spiritual warfare, we talk about theology and theological reflection from the beginning of the mentoring ministry, and we reinforce their significance throughout the mentoring season. Initially, the word *theology* was intimidating to some mentees. They felt that it was an academic word with little practical bearing on real life. And some women were unsure if the study of theology was really for them. These inaccurate conclusions are evidence of the spiritual battles waging in our minds and are part of the reason we give up so easily and are defeated when under spiritual attack.

I've found there is no need for women to fear learning about theology. Theology is simply our foundational beliefs about God.[7] Sound theology helps us renew our minds, take a stand against Satan and his schemes, and respond rightly in the world. As disciples of Christ, we need intentional theological reflection. We need sound theology! Author Carolyn Custis James writes, "Every woman's first and highest calling is to become a great theologian. For all of us, nothing approaches the importance or the urgency of pursuing a deeper knowledge of God—a knowledge that makes thinkers and doers out of all of us."[8] Carolyn frequently lectures that we are all theologians—we all have beliefs about God and the world around us. What matters is whether we are good theologians or bad ones. Whether we commit to renew our minds is of concern in matters of war.

Whether we commit to disciple our minds is also of concern in matters of love. In the heart of every good theologian is the desire to know God and please him. We obey God because we love him.[9] These truths are inseparable and impossible without the divine revelation of the Holy Spirit. The ministry of the Holy Spirit enables us to recognize and acknowledge our human condition. As several church confessions state, "We confess that we are in bondage to sin and cannot free ourselves. We have sinned against you [God] in thought, word, and deed. We have not loved you with our whole heart; we have not loved our neighbors as ourselves."[10] The Word of God and the Holy Spirit help us recognize that our human condition is fallen, corrupted by sin.[11] Prior to placing our faith in Christ, we were incapable of understanding or submitting to the will of the Lord because we were slaves to sin. Not only were we slaves, but we delighted in our bondage. Our sinful desires were incapable of leading us to obedience. But the love of Christ compels us to discipline ourselves and submit to his work of transformation in our minds and souls.

This discipline is initiated by God through Christ and the power of the Holy Spirit that changes hearts and transforms lives. We have Christ as our best example of how to live in loving devotion to God. Christ understood the mind of his Father, and he obeyed. Christ is *God with us* offering the gift of salvation, while the Holy Spirit is *God in us* as a result of accepting his gracious gift. The Holy Spirit within us activates our mind's knowledge of God. It then gives us power to faithfully walk in victory over any spiritual battle and in loving obedience to God's will. Living our lives on purpose means we live free from the bondage of sin and in generous service to God and others.[12] The Holy Spirit is the great protagonist of theological reflection, helping us to better understand the world in which we live and the spiritual powers at work around us.

Through mentoring, we invite the powerful work of the Holy Spirit to retrain the way we think, and that develops in us a holistic and active theology and Christian worldview that stands against the schemes and messages of this world. Intentionally developing a Christian worldview means that we acknowledge the changes in time and culture in light of the biblical truth we know. Theological reflection challenges us so that biblical truth dictates how we respond rightly in the world. Through reflection, we learn to listen to Jesus, who said, "*If* you hold to my teachings, you are *really* my disciples. *Then* you will know the truth, and the truth will set you free."[13]

So what does theological reflection and developing a Christian worldview look like in a mentoring group? Theological reflection often begins by asking the right questions. Through mentoring, we cultivate our minds and explore the answers to life's important questions with the reading, study, and understanding of God's Word as our foundation.

The Discipline of Bible Reading and Bible Study

Godly mentors must be lovers of the Word of God. Years of challenges, sound teaching, and encouragement have nurtured this love in my own life. I once heard someone say, "Everyone needs to complete *wide* studies. This is when they read or go through large portions of Scripture just to get a feel for God's story, while at the same time they complete *deep* studies, and this is when readers focus on better understanding certain chunks of the Bible." I agree with this. We need studies of the Word that give us a better understanding of God's big picture—his redemptive plan for the world—and we need focused and practical studies to help us face the challenges of the day.

The truth is, God wins, yet "many Christians are losing the day spiritually because they are not connecting with God through His Word regularly."[14] Therefore, I encourage you to incorporate the reading and study of God's Word into your mentoring group. The Center for Bible Engagement completed a report including an online survey of over forty thousand Americans (from eight years old to eighty) titled "Understanding the Bible Engagement Challenge: Scientific Evidence for the Power of 4."

The report revealed that in the general population, ages eighteen to twenty-four, 10.5% of people read or listened to the Bible four to seven days per week (71.3% reported not reading the Bible at all).

10.5%. Pause and think about that for a moment.

Of people age twenty-five or older, 18.2% read the Bible four to seven days per week (with 62.1% reporting not reading the Bible at all).[15] If that doesn't alarm you, the numbers among self-identified born again Christians are equally as troubling. Among professing Christians, 29.2% of eighteen- to twenty-four-year-olds reported reading their Bibles four to seven days per week (39.1% reported not reading their Bibles at all), and 39.2% of self-identified Christians age twenty-five and older reported reading their Bibles four to seven days per week (with 29.1% reporting not reading their Bibles at all).[16]

Press pause again. A large number of professing Christians age eighteen and above reported not reading their Bibles at all!

Why does this matter? "Without a firm grasp of the Bible, nurtured through daily reading or listening, we weaken our ability to defend the faith we claim, [are] less confident to share that faith with others, and [are] more vulnerable to falling prey to false teachings."[17] Most important, we miss the opportunity to encounter the living God. Jesus Christ is present to each of us through the reading of Scripture by the power of the Holy Spirit.

The report does conclude with several encouraging statistics, however, which I hope will motivate you to accept the challenge to disciple fragile minds to love the study of God's Word. It tells us that Christians who are engaged in Scripture most days of the week have lower odds of participating in these destructive behaviors:

- Getting drunk = 57% lower odds
- Having sex outside marriage = 68% lower odds
- Engaging with pornography = 61% lower odds
- Gambling = 74% lower odds

In addition, those who read or listen to the Bible at least four days a week have higher odds of participating in these kingdom-minded behaviors:

- Sharing faith with others = 228% higher odds
- Discipling others = 231% higher odds
- Memorizing Scripture = 407% higher odds[18]

Do you want to see more women living holy lives of freedom? Do you want people of God sharing their faith, discipling others, and memorizing Scripture? If so, you must equip them to read and study the Word of God. Bible engagement is a significant means by which God transforms lives. Not only does Bible engagement help us know God and renew our minds, this study suggests that consistently interacting with Scripture for four or more days a week can serve as a spiritual shield of protection for us in spiritual battle.19

Mentoring challenges and equips us to disciple our minds. This transformation and renewal begins by grounding ourselves in God's Word. So grab your Bible, select a great mentoring resource, and get started!

Mentor for Life

1. Prior to reading this chapter, what were your initial thoughts concerning theology? How has this chapter challenged the way you think about theology?

2. Is reading the Bible part of your daily routine? Now that you understand the benefits of Bible engagement, how can you practically make this discipline a priority in your life?

3. Get your mind right: What three resources might you consider to challenge you and your mentees concerning the mentoring pillars: *knowing and loving God, knowing your identity in Christ, and loving your neighbor?*[20]

4. Are you aware of any injustices or needs in your local community? Prayerfully consider one issue your mentoring group might focus on addressing together during your mentoring season. Ask: What are the issues? What community issue(s) is your church addressing? What workers, community servants, and nonprofit organizations are addressing the issues?

5. Discipline Exercise: Write a one-page theological statement (with supporting Scripture references) communicating what it means to live as a follower of Christ. Consider how this document can be a tool to educate and encourage your mentees concerning right thinking and right actions.

6. Summarize in four or five sentences what you have learned from this chapter.

Tweet This

Discipleship of the Mind: "Transformation begins in the mind. Right thinking produces right actions." #Mentor4Life @asistasjourney

Eight

Discipleship of the Soul

If God is speaking, then nothing else matters but listening!
Brennan Manning[1]

I was afraid. I sat on the floor with my back against the couch, twirled the pen in my hands, and waited patiently for all eyes to turn in my direction. The women's ministry leadership team at our church was gathered for our annual fall retreat, and the speaker had asked us to think about a question. It was simple enough: "What do you want us to pray about for you this year?" The response that welled up within me was frightening.

"Brokenness," I said.

It was 2011, and I had just finished a seminary assignment reading of Peter Scazzero's book *Emotionally Healthy Spirituality*. Scazzero writes about brokenness on a level I hadn't previously considered: "A broken person . . . is so secure in the love of God that she is unable to be insulted. When criticized, judged, or insulted, she thinks to herself, *'It is far worse than you think!'*"[2] After reading these words, I wondered, "Am I unoffendable?" Far worse than the answer to that question were the feelings of sadness and disgust from the sinking realization that if I was criticized, judged, or insulted, my heart's response would be, "I'm not that bad." I knew I needed a deeper level of self-awareness, and the only way to get there was through seeing my own sinfulness and welcoming this kind of brokenness.

I cried out to God for mercy and asked for prayer from my sisters in leadership. God did not take long to answer. Within three months, my family experienced the loss of two of its members and my marriage was suddenly heading toward a dead end. Emotions overflowed. Grief. Hurt. Anger. "Offendedness." My soul was weary. But God used the spiritual disciplines presented in this chapter and the stern and loving hand of a mentor to lead me through a spiritual wilderness.

Discipline to Pray

The first discipline we often turn to is that of prayer. I won't spend time covering the "why" and "how" of prayer because many books discuss the topic at length.[3] I simply want to encourage you not to overlook this basic spiritual practice or assume that mentees understand or embrace the significance of it. We know that the disciples asked Jesus to teach them how to pray; therefore, prayer is an important spiritual discipline and practice for mentoring.[4]

In a mentoring relationship, we learn to pray because we realize we are in desperate need of God and in desperate need of change. Through prayer, we humble ourselves and allow our needs to shape the motivations of our hearts.[5] Richard J. Foster writes, "Prayer is the central avenue God uses to transform us. If we are unwilling to change, we will soon stop praying. Praying will no longer be a noticeable characteristic of our lives. When we see our need as it truly is, we are motivated to draw near to the heartbeat of God and this increases our desire to be conformed to Christ."[6]

Through mentoring, we learn how to pray for change in ourselves, but a significant part of our mentoring group gatherings is also devoted to intercessory prayer for each other. I was always thankful for and encouraged by my ministry partner, Nikki, who was committed to daily interceding for me and the other mentors on our leadership team. She would rise at 5:00 a.m. so she could review our prayer requests before going to work. She looked up Scripture and prayed scriptural prayers over us. Why? She said, "The end result of intercession for me was not only a closer walk with my Lord, but also a dependence upon him to provide answers. Additionally, intercession provided a spiritual connection and closer relationship with each of the mentors on our leadership team."

It is both humbling and comforting to know that someone is always lifting you up in prayer. As mentors, we need to commit to intercessory prayer for those we mentor with the understanding that God hears our prayers, cares about the things that concern our hearts, and promises to answer.[7]

Discipline to Fast

The discipline of fasting is less commonly understood and practiced. Dr. Tony Evans defines fasting as:

> The deliberate abstinence from some form of physical gratification, for a period of time, in order to achieve a great spiritual goal. Fasting usually involves setting aside food, although we can fast from any physical appetite, including sex within marriage (1 Corinthians 7:5). . . . The idea is to devote the time we would ordinarily spend on these activities to prayer and waiting before the Lord. Fasting calls us to renounce the natural in order to invoke the supernatural.[8]

For some, the challenge seems too great, and there are sometimes concerns about health or how to effectively practice this discipline.[9] Note that fasting is not a commandment or something we are required to do as Christians. Remember, the spiritual disciplines are not practices of a new covenantal law. They are a means of God's grace meant to set us free from our own bondage and self-absorption. They are a means of discipline for our souls.

Through its narratives, the Bible presents several reasons for the people of God to fast. Old Testament prophets often called a community to fasting, prayer, and lament as a humble response to tragedy. Believers in the New Testament fasted to seek God's holy presence and direction for important decisions.[10] Fasting also seemed to accompany the call to public ministry—a practice entered into through a wilderness or crossroads experience—as was the case with Jesus and the apostle Paul.[11] During the Sermon on the Mount, Jesus gives instruction on *"when* you fast . . ." (Matt. 6:16). He is assuming, in saying "when," that his disciples would continue the spiritual discipline of fasting after his ascension.[12] Jesus' teaching on fasting is within "the context of his teaching on giving and praying. It is as if there is an almost unconscious assumption that giving, praying, and fasting are all part of Christian devotion."[13] For all these reasons, the discipline of fasting is worth our consideration.

We commit to fasting as an act of humility, recognizing our desperate need for God. When we fast, our motivation is not to manipulate God, earn his favor, or bargain for results.[14] True biblical fasting is for a specific spiritual purpose and is often accompanied by prayer. If you are in the midst of a spiritual struggle, that would be a good reason to consider fasting. If a mentee is seeking direction or lacks clarity on a particular issue, that could also be a reason to fast. If a community is grieving or in mourning, a communal fast would be an appropriate sacred response.

Christians may wish to fast when confronted with what Dr. Scot McKnight refers to as *"grievous sacred moments."* According to Dr. McKnight, fasting is "a person's whole-body, natural response to life's sacred moments."[15] What I love about this definition is that Dr. McKnight is not asking us to contemplate whether we should fast. He is asking us to consider what would prompt us to fast. By encouraging us to identify a "grievous sacred moment," McKnight is essentially asking, "What areas in your life or what observations in this world are so bad that they prompt you to turn your plate over and get on your knees?" By humbling ourselves to pray and committing to the discipline of fasting, we are engaging the whole self—body and soul—in a spiritual action that becomes sacred. If nothing in our lives breaks us in this way, perhaps that's an indicator that either we are not paying attention or we have not humbled ourselves before the Lord.

Fasting renews our minds and draws us near to God. Dr. Tony Evans writes, "Since you can't have a face-to-face conversation with Jesus today, fasting is a way you can make a special link with him when you need a spiritual breakthrough in your life."[16] When accompanied by prayer and intentional reading, fasting can become a *place of conversion* with God. Fasting is an empty soul's cry to a holy God, and we are prompted to fast when we accept that only a miraculous, spiritual encounter with God will rightfully shape our hearts concerning a grievous event or a right action. If we don't take the time to recognize our desperate need for God in light of horrific situations, we become blind and our hearts can grow numb to the evil around us. Not only does fasting allow us to grieve the sins of this world, it also allows us to grieve our own personal sins—both the wrong actions we do and the right actions we fail to take.

In this way, fasting shapes our character and centers us to focus on God. It makes us more compassionate so we can love our neighbors well. Through fasting, we become more humble, aware, and compassionate. Therefore, fasting is not something we should fear or shy away from simply because we have not done it before.[17] You can practice this discipline with your mentees, and it can be a powerful experience for you and for them.

Discipline to Journal

If the disciplines of prayer and fasting encourage our souls to become poor in spirit, then journaling reminds us of that spiritual poverty. I previously mentioned a season of brokenness in my life, a time when I prayed and fasted consistently. In addition to those disciplines, I wrote weekly journal entries to my mentor, who walked with me through the experience. Journaling encouraged personal reflection and allowed me to take a humble seat at the Lord's feet. An excerpt from my journal reminded me of my spiritual condition during that wilderness experience:

> *February 6, 2012*
>
> *How can a person be so secure in the love of God that she is unable to be insulted? God is speaking to me about living in his grace. What does that really mean? The spiritual director at seminary assured me that I still have so much more grace to experience. He also encouraged me to pray for God's mercy. God have mercy on me, a sinner.*
>
> *When the Israelites were offended, they grumbled against Moses, and in return, Moses grumbled against God. Yet Moses continued with the people. He pleaded for God's love, grace, and mercy on their behalf. God offered forgiveness. So, in my broken condition, prayer is in order, not only for myself and my family, but also for my local congregation and God's universal church.*
>
> *I plead for God's love, grace, and mercy, and enter the Lord's presence understanding that brokenness is not something I can do of my own will; it is a miraculous work of God. In this week's reading, Dr. Tony Evans wrote, "to be broken means to be stripped of your self-sufficiency."[18] I need thee, oh God. You must become greatest, I must become least.*

During this time, God was shaping my heart and preparing me to lead with more grace. Through personal reflection, spiritual discipline, and the accountability of a mentor, he was chipping away at my false sense of self. This is why I encourage journaling as an effective mentoring tool. Journaling enables us to listen to our own hearts, and helps us see and understand ourselves more clearly. Richard J. Foster concludes, "One of the principle objects of our study should be ourselves. We should learn the things that control *us*. . . . What controls our moods? Why do we like certain people and dislike others? What do these things teach us about ourselves?"[19] Journaling helps us confront and process these character-defining issues.

Journaling is also a way of taking what we are learning about God and making it personal. In light of our mentoring commitments, journaling gives us the opportunity to answer the question, "What does this (e.g., teaching, theology position, injustice, or concern) mean to me?" This is when journaling becomes a *place of conversion*. Yet journaling is more than a personal mentoring exercise; it is an act of trust. "Like all spiritual disciplines, it begins with the trust that God is active at the heart of our lives and the life of the world. It begins with our openness to trusting in the transforming power of Christ's Spirit to lead us closer to our true selves and to God."[20] Through mentoring, we can grow in our trust of God and understanding of self by disciplining ourselves to write.

Discipline to Retreat

We are human. Our fleshly bodies get tired, and sometimes we need to rest. Intentionally setting aside time to do so prevents burnout and ensures we can give a more gracious and humble presentation of ourselves to the world. Unfortunately, unhealthy and unrealistic expectations still exist that women will somehow get everything done while endlessly pouring into the lives of others without ever taking time to rejuvenate themselves. This is not how God wants us to operate. The Sabbath is a wonderful reminder that we all need weekly times when we stop and rest. This is the way God designed humans to live.

A careful study of biblical leaders, including Jesus, reveals a consistent pattern in their lives. They regularly drew away to secluded places free from distractions to be with God. Today, we call this practice a spiritual retreat. Concerning retreats, Foster wrote, "I have discovered that the most difficult problem is not finding the time but convincing myself that this is important enough to set aside the time."[21] Let me assure you—it is indeed important to set aside time for personal retreat. You can retreat to experience solitude and silence, to engage in prayer or devoted times of study, or to clear your mind so you can better prioritize, vision cast, and plan. You can even take a retreat so you can catch up on rest or use the potty without interruption. There is no single right reason to go on a spiritual retreat. The encouragement is simply that you commit to go and trust that God will meet you in those sacred moments.

In my experience, the primary reason women don't retreat is guilt. This is especially true if they are mothers. It can be like pulling teeth trying to gather women for a spiritual retreat. Some refuse to stop work while others simply cannot fathom being away from their families for a whole day. Others find the idea downright selfish. Regardless of these opinions, God has designed humans for sacred rhythms that include rest. Whether it's a spiritual retreat, a spiritually engaging and nurturing conference, a fellowship dinner, or a girls' night on the town, taking time to rest, relax, and focus on the Lord is important for our souls' care. We must make life-giving choices to rest and retreat so we can faithfully continue our work and live our lives on purpose for God. Cultivating this discipline may take some creative thinking and planning. Perhaps this is a discipline your mentoring group can discuss and support together.

This Is How We Do It

How do all these disciplines of the soul relate to mentoring? By cultivating spiritual disciplines in a mentoring ministry, we remove the false expectations that "we can do it all" without prioritizing our personal relationship with the Lord. Together, we humble ourselves with healthy reminders that we are not God, and we are in desperate need of him. "For in him we live and move and have our being" (Acts 17:28). Although we gather together only once a month, we also cultivate these disciplines through mentoring exercises which become a *place of conversion* for each of us. We encourage and celebrate these spiritual disciplines of the mind and soul as healthy and sustaining life choices.

As you can see, the commitment to a mentoring group is a humble commitment to learning, teaching, and growing together. A mentoring group is more than just Bible study, questions, and conversations. Selecting a theme of focus and outlining a curriculum that guides our mentoring community for the entire season shows intentionality. The Bible is our foundation for growing in truth, trust, and understanding of God.

You will need to prayerfully incorporate the best use of the Word in your ministry context and mentoring relationships. As a ministry leader, I do not outline a generic Bible study plan for all the women involved in our mentoring ministry, because everyone is at a different place in their spiritual journey. Some mentees already have daily reading routines or participate in other Bible studies or small groups. This may be the case in your ministry context as well, so I encourage you to resist the temptation to add unnecessary burdens to those who already have good Bible-engaging habits. Additionally, you want to challenge and not overwhelm the women who are just getting started with Bible reading. In short, the mentor must be attentive and work with her mentees to develop this discipline.

For the purpose of discipling the mind, we intentionally make a careful selection of three mentoring resources (which often reference larger portions of Scripture and make the practical application connection for the reader). These mentoring resources, which progressively address the three pillars of the mentoring framework, form the foundation for all of our learning, including Scripture memorization, Bible reading, journal prompts, and exercises. Therefore, the preparation and commitments women make in their places of conversion outside of their group gatherings are just as important as their group participation and attendance. We have seen transformation occur *only* when women commit to both. Through these commitments, the mentoring group becomes a community of learning, affirmation, accountability, and support.

For Scripture memorization, we select two passages per month (normally one from each testament) that complement the reading, and the women memorize these passages together. Scripture memorization is important because as disciples of Christ, we want God's Word to become a part of us (John 1:1–4, 14). One mentor told me that she once knew a woman, Mrs. Robertson, who was ninety-four years old. This wise woman said she was so very grateful to have hidden God's Word in her heart when she was young because, in her old age, her eyes no longer allowed her to read. Memorizing Scripture does hide God's Word in our hearts, and it conditions our souls to live in a manner that pleases the Lord.[22]

In addition to Bible reading and Scripture memorization, we teach women how to pray. It is unwise to assume those you mentor know how. Some women can't find the words to pray or feel like they don't know what to say. Others may question the need for prayer. Still others lack confidence in praying out loud. Through mentoring, we challenge women to go before the throne of grace where they will receive mercy from God. In our mentoring community, we teach healthy practices of confession and repentance, as well as how to become peacemakers, extend forgiveness to others, and reconcile relationships. These practices flow out of the discipline of prayer.

Intercession is also a crucial part of our ministry. At the first mentoring group gathering, each attendee is given the opportunity to share one prayer request they want the group to pray about for the entire mentoring season.[23] Additionally, they share one prayer request per month, followed by updates on how God has answered previous prayer requests. These requests should generally be about the mentees themselves, not generic petitions or matters concerning others. There will be appropriate times for sharing other concerns, but participating in intercession is one of the quickest ways to know someone's heart and become intimately connected.

We limit the prayer request to one because as a ministry mentor reminded our leadership team, "I don't want the ladies in my mentoring group spending more time sharing requests than they are actually praying." When requests are shared, all mentors and mentees document them and commit to praying throughout the month. Praying the Scriptures has become an anchor in our ministry, and therefore, we search the Bible for Scriptures to pray in connection to the requests. Additionally, we include a column in our prayer journal where we record how God answers our prayers.[24] Both personal prayer and intercession can be accompanied by fasting.

Finally, we schedule occasional spiritual retreats that offer women opportunities to practice the disciplines of silence, solitude, and rest. Let me encourage you to be proactive with this pursuit. Research local retreat opportunities so you have information readily available for yourself, your leadership team, your mentees, and any other person who may need it. Consider scheduling a set time when several women can retreat together, even if the time is largely spent in solitude. Who knows when God may ask you to bless someone with the precious gift of rest?

I share these spiritual disciplines and practices not as a model you must follow step-by-step, but as examples to inspire your own creative ideas that best fit your ministry context. As disciples, we long to cultivate a disciplined life that rearranges our priorities and regularly ushers us into the Lord's presence.[25] Our minds and souls need discipline. After all, it is true—we become what we worship.

Mentor for Life

1. Before reading this chapter, what were some of your opinions concerning the spiritual disciplines of prayer, fasting, journaling, and retreat? Do you regularly practice any of these disciplines? If so, how have the disciplines contributed to transformation in your life? If not, what has hindered your ability to embrace a spiritual discipline? Explain how your opinion has changed concerning any of these disciplines.

2. In what ways might God be inviting you to experience more of his grace and mercy?

3. How is God calling you, as a mentor, to respond as a result of reading this chapter? Given your ministry context and relationships, what spiritual disciplines might you study and practice in the future?

4. What spiritual disciplines might you practice with your mentoring group? Why do you believe these disciplines will be beneficial to you and your mentees?

5. Discipline Exercise: As a journaling experience, contemplate answers to the following questions: What controls you? What controls your moods or makes you angry? "Why do you like certain people and dislike others?"[26] Where do you invest the majority of your time? How do you spend the money God has provided for you? What do these things teach you about yourself?

6. Summarize in four or five sentences what you have learned from this chapter.

Tweet This

"Spiritual disciplines invite us into the Lord's presence to embrace our true selves so we can live authentically and love others well." #Mentor4Life @asistasjourney

Mentoring

A Commitment to God's Mission

> *Mission is the people of God intentionally crossing barriers*
> *from the church to the nonchurch, faith to nonfaith,*
> *to proclaim by word and deed*
> *the coming of the kingdom of God*
> *in Jesus Christ;*
> *this task is achieved by means of the church's participation*
> *in God's mission of reconciling people*
> *to God, to themselves, to each other, and to the world,*
> *and gathering them into the church*
> *through repentance and faith in Jesus Christ*
> *by the work of the Holy Spirit*
> *with a view to the transformation of the world*
> *as a sign of the coming of the kingdom*
> *in Jesus Christ.*
>
> *Charles Van Engen*[1]

Understanding God's kingdom mission gives us an urgency and intentionality to run our spiritual race, and to invite others to win on the journey of following Christ.

Mentoring as intentional discipleship requires that we focus on God's kingdom mission and understand the felt needs of others.

Nine

Mission Accomplishment

Anyone who is willing to follow Christ can become a mighty influence on the world providing, of course, this person has the proper training.
Robert E. Coleman[1]

Here we go. On a run. Just for fun. Oh yeah. Delayed cadence count cadence Marines cadence count . . . 1-can't hear you . . . 2-a little louder . . . 3-all together . . . 4-much better . . . 1-hit it, 2-hit it, 3-hit it, 4-hit it . . . 1, 2, 3, 4, United States Marine Corps.

Oh, how I loved waking up for an early morning run. There is nothing like starting the day with the cool breeze on your face and the loud shouts of motivated Marines in your ears. I'm sure many of my fellow Marines struggled with this activity, but personally, I loved training along the waterfronts of Camp Lejeune, North Carolina, feeling my heart pounding inside my chest and knowing that as Marines, we had already started our day with gusto while many people were still snuggled in their beds. Our reward? Watching God lift the sun into the morning sky just as we neared the end of our run.

My love of running and my hunger to meet with God in this way began early. From the age of eleven, I enjoyed competitive racing. Track and field was my primary focus, but I also ran cross-country to stay in shape during the off-season. By the time I entered high school, winning had become a habit for me. During my junior year, our track teams were the best in the state of South Carolina. The following year, I broke the school record and won gold in the state championship for my featured event, the 100-meter hurdles. After being rewarded with four varsity letters in cross-country, four varsity letters in track and field, breaking a school record, and earning gold at the state level, people started referring to me as a "star athlete."

But that wasn't how I saw myself. Winning was simply part of my "mission," as the crucial goal in my life at that point was earning a full scholarship to attend a great college. I saw that through my love of running and the gifts God had given me, I had opportunities to learn, grow, and expand the possibilities for my future.

In the last chapter, we talked about our need to rest. In the midst of busy schedules, we need to intentionally carve out time to retreat and recharge. Our human needs, good stewardship, and our focus on God's kingdom mission, however, require us to work before we can rest. In the same way that going for an early morning run can be part of a long-term goal or bigger life plan, disciples of Christ must see their daily work and commitments (no matter how small) as part of God's wider mission for the world. Understanding God's kingdom mission gives us an urgency and intentionality to run our own spiritual race, and to invite others on the journey of following Christ with us.

On Winning in Life

Great athletes—those who excel and win—are people who work hard. They get up earlier, stay later, and tend to be more passionate and focused than their competitors. When we are well prepared and well rested, winning looks easy. While the casual observer knows how to recognize greatness, she doesn't always see the behind-the-scene efforts that go into making someone "great." Those who watched me win a race weren't there to see the hours and miles spent running on the cross-country team just to stay in shape (because I loathed long distance running). They didn't know I was one of the few girls allowed to lift weights with the basketball and football teams after school. They didn't see the countless practices where I ran sprint drills, putting forth a tenacious effort to beat the guys. They didn't see the hours after track practices where I learned and perfected proper hurdle techniques with a college athlete's help. Perseverance, stamina, discipline, repetition, and technique all reflected my urgent desire to win, and my intentional, focused training made me a great athlete.

I love that when we read the Scriptures, we find the apostle Paul using athletic metaphors to help us better understand the process of growing and maturing as followers of Christ. Paul ministered in a society that highly valued sports, physical prowess, and strict training; therefore, he understood that to speak of God's kingdom mission as a spiritual race was a comparison his audience would understand. It was natural for him to challenge his readers with this teaching in 1 Corinthians 9:24–27:

> Do you not know that in a race all the runners run, but only one gets the prize? Run in such a way as to get the prize. Everyone who competes in the games goes into strict training. They do it to get a crown that will not last, but we do it to get a crown that will last forever. Therefore I do not run like someone running aimlessly; I do not fight like a man beating the air. No, I strike a blow to my body and make it my slave so that after I have preached to others, I myself will not be disqualified for the prize.[2]

Here, Paul is communicating the simple truth that not everybody gets a trophy. I'm sorry if that hurts people's feelings, but that's how things are in the real world!

When we commit to being disciples of Jesus, we accept a mission from God. Our lives are reset on a proper course to win our spiritual race, but we must still run that race! We have not yet reached the finish line. In the same way we make physical sacrifices for our health and wellness or even for our vanity, we must also make sacrifices to persevere in our spiritual race. I'm saddened by the thought of Christian women who run aimlessly, who fight as if they are boxing the air. They need someone to challenge and motivate them to discipline themselves and focus so they can receive their eternal prize of life—a crown from God that will last forever.[3] Perseverance is the mark of our faith!

Some people want all the benefits of being a disciple of Christ but none of the responsibility. In our culture of celebrating individualism, we each want our brand of Jesus as we insist on doing things our own way. We don't want to commit to the body of Christ. We are content with a "discipleship" that simply asks us to show up for Sunday morning worship or Bible study or maybe a community fellowship or small group. Since we have other "more important" things to do, we want a faith calling composed of small commitments and short timeframes. Let us remember, however, the empire of Rome was not built in one day. The fact that Christ has not yet returned means there is still important work needed to advance his kingdom on earth, and he is advancing it in and through us. The problem is, of course, that people who claim to know and love God don't always want to make long-term investments in his kingdom. Discipleship is not something we simply show up for or something we do one time. Discipleship is a journey, not a destination. Dr. Tony Evans writes:

> Discipleship is a process, not an event. Thus it demands spiritual growth. The formula is simple: Rate multiplied by time equals distance. The speed at which you move given the time that you have been saved will determine the spiritual distance you cover. This is why you can have Christians who have been

saved five years who are more spiritually mature and better disciples of Christ than others who have been Christians for twenty-five years. They have moved at a faster pace within the time period since their conversion.[4]

The urgency of God's kingdom mission compels us to intentional discipleship. My vision is to share the message that we have been freely saved by the grace of God, not to pursue our own individualistic and selfish agendas, but to be empowered by the Holy Spirit to run and win our own spiritual race. This race is not an easy run. It is a faith journey that stretches us beyond our human limitations and understanding, and it certainly stretches us beyond our comfort level. To win, we must constantly consider the cost of discipleship.

The apostle Paul writes that each believer in Christ should engage in rigorous training and run as if they want to get the prize. Though I excelled in track sprints as an athlete, I've learned that the Christian race is more like those long distance cross-country miles. Running long spiritual miles builds endurance,[5] and once we develop stamina, we can race through the daily sprints as if our lives depend on it, because they do!

Intentional, Focused Training

When I offer leadership training, my goal is to help potential mentors understand they have a faithful contribution to make to God's kingdom mission. Mentors set the direction and help guide those in their care. We are like coaches, modeling (however imperfectly) a life of *being* in Christ. We invite others to join us on this faith journey, help them discern their purpose and calling, and equip them to respond in obedience.

How do we do this? It begins by remembering that mentoring as intentional discipleship is God's mission. We help women learn to embrace the *whole gospel* and allow that embrace to saturate every aspect of their lives. The gospel, when properly understood, will change our priorities and enable us to live lives that are sacrificial offerings to God (2 Tim. 4:6–8). In our prayers, we remind ourselves of who God is and what he has done for us, and we look forward with hope to the glorious day of Christ's return. Until that day, we commit to fight the good fight, to finish the race, and to keep the faith. We help women see where their lives and their God-given missions fit into the larger picture of what God is accomplishing through Christ, between his first and second coming. We do this by selflessly giving ourselves in relationship so the truth of God's Word and the love of Christ can take root in our hearts and theirs as we come together.

Mentoring on God's Mission

Launching a mentoring ministry was challenging. My family was new to the area and new to the church. We didn't know anyone yet, so I hadn't had significant interaction with many of the women in the congregation. Additionally, I was younger than the median age of the church membership. In spite of these challenges, I was committed to making disciples of Jesus Christ. I knew I was called to this kingdom work, so I accepted the responsibility and began with the following two leadership fundamentals:

- All great leaders mentor. Mentoring is an integral part of leadership.
- Mentoring is crucial to successfully accomplishing any mission.

Let's unpack these fundamentals. For me, they are connected to the concepts of *mission accomplishment* and *troop welfare*. In the military, there is always a clear objective, and when you have reached your goal, you have successfully accomplished your mission. In the church, we can define mission accomplishment as making and multiplying disciples of Jesus Christ for the purpose of glorifying God and advancing His kingdom agenda.

Troop welfare is a concept that reminds us that the success of our mission is largely dependent on the holistic well-being of the service men and women. How are the troops doing? Are they healthy? Are they physically fit? Are their families taken care of? Are they ready for battle? Are they prepared to engage the enemy? In the church, this means we intentionally establish God-centered relationships by prayerfully and intentionally calling people to follow Jesus, compassionately teaching and training them along the way, and equipping them for works of service in God's kingdom.

Mission Accomplishment: It's Purposeful

Whether you are thinking about launching a mentoring small group within your home or starting a mentoring ministry in your local church, your purpose must be clear. My deep conviction from the beginning was that our church needed a mentoring ministry that was intentional and holistic—a ministry wherein a team of mentors could be trained to make disciples of Jesus Christ and who commit to God's kingdom mission of transforming the world. This led me to define mentoring in the following way:

Mentoring is a trusted partnership where people share wisdom that fosters spiritual growth and leads to transformation, as mentors and disciples grow in their love of Christ, knowledge of self, and love of others.

With this definition in place, our team understood that mission accomplishment or ministry "success" meant lives transformed into Christ's image. Our goal wasn't a large ministry or having a certain number of women in each mentoring group. Winning was about God's kingdom mission. Winning was about seeing his work accomplished through the life transformation of all participants.

The Bible reveals that this kind of transformation is God's work of the heart—something only God can do. It is best reflected in our posture toward God and our relationships with other people. So while God needs to do the miraculous spiritual work of transformation, we can submit by teaching and encouraging women to assume a posture of receptivity to God. If we are not changing and growing in our understanding of who God is, if we are not surrendered to being changed by him, and if our relationships only bear the fruit of brokenness, unforgiveness, and bitterness, lacking Christian love and peace, we have to question whether our church is truly engaging in God's mission of making disciples. My hope is that the lessons and stories shared here will inspire and equip you to know God's kingdom mission and to commit your life, ministry, and work to that mission. Let's do the work God wants us to do and stop questioning whether we are actually making disciples who truly follow Jesus.

Mentors have a responsibility to those in their care. They need to keep their disciples (mentees) focused on God's kingdom purposes. Because our culture is primarily focused on all of us meeting our own needs, we should begin by helping mentees understand that being a disciple of Christ is not about getting what we want, it's about pursuing *God's* desires for his kingdom. Our culture encourages us to have an attitude of "Me first," but the Bible reveals that attitude as a reflection of a sinful heart. The sinful heart demands what it wants, often without knowing what it *truly* needs (Rom. 8:26). Mentoring calls people to pursue a narrow course that is countercultural. This will reset their priorities, train their hearts to lean toward God, and point them in the right direction. Mentors can confront this spiritual tension head-on and follow God's agenda by looking to Jesus and his relationship with the twelve disciples. As Regi Campbell wonderfully explains:

> Everything about what He did was about *His agenda*, not theirs. Jesus didn't worry about being an inconvenience to His mentorees. He knew he was giving them the chance of a lifetime by allowing them to follow and learn from Him. . . .

Jesus invited them to follow Him, and they did. They left their businesses, their wives (at least in Peter's case), and their families to take Jesus up on His offer to become 'fishers of men.'[6]

Jesus was the mentor, and the twelve disciples followed his agenda not because he lorded his leadership over them, but because he served them. He understood the big picture, kept it in view, and was mentoring them with his Father's purpose, mission, and goals in mind. They mutually undertood and accepted that Jesus was their rabbi—there to teach and train them. Jesus understood the mission, so he could look beyond the daily circumstances of life and constantly point his disciples to the finish line of the race.

In a nutshell, that's what mentors must do. They set the course and train their mentees to see that their daily situations are actually part of a longer race they are called to run with perseverance, stamina, and discipline (James 1:2–4). Through regular teaching and training that includes loving and accountable relationships, prayer, intentional reading, Bible engagement, and service work, mentors keep their mentees focused on God's mission by motivating them to continue on their Christian race. Perseverance builds our character, guarantees our maturity, and affirms our hope.

"The greater danger for most of us lies not in setting our aim too high and falling short; but in setting our aim too low, and achieving our mark."

Michelangelo

If all this sounds like a bit too much, let me encourage you to raise the bar higher than you are accustomed. The truth is, people learn to persevere when expectations are high. When folks clearly see what the stakes are, and they really want to win, they actively respond. Visionary goals and high expectations draw us in to depend on God, challenge us to take an honest look at ourselves, and give us confidence and courage to step out and strategically take kingdom-size risks in faith. Disciples of Christ *should* be the most active, engaging, and innovative people in the world! Olympic athletes understand that if they want to take home the gold, they have to earn it. We are God's spiritual Olympians. Our salvation gets us into the games, and our work makes us a victorious people. So when we commit to mentor, we commit to aim high.

Gracefully Living the Mission Together

Mentors must aim for integrity in their practical living. Daily we are called to surrender our lives, passions, and desires to God with a clear conscience, knowing that God's grace is present to meet us when we fail. Through mentoring, we encourage one another, spurring each other on to love, respond rightly, do good works, and live on mission for God. This need for accountability and integrity is an area where the church can use some motivation. Rule setting just leaves people feeling inadequate and guilty. Rules make it acceptable for the self-righteous to judge and for degenerates to pass blame. Rules do not nurture God-honoring relationships. Living by the rules is its own false religion.

On the other hand, the apostles[7] and leaders throughout church history had staunch warnings against living double lives and abusing the grace of God. The sin of hypocrisy is perhaps the worst slight to the church and does not promote the true gospel of Jesus. In his classic work, *The Cost of Discipleship*, the abuse of grace and willful sin was one of Dietrich Bonhoeffer's chief concerns. He wrote:

> Cheap grace is the deadly enemy of our Church . . . [cheap] grace amounts to the justification of sin without the justification of the repentant sinner who departs from sin and from whom sin departs . . . Cheap grace is the preaching of forgiveness without requiring repentance, baptism without church

discipline, Communion without confession, absolution without personal confession. Cheap grace is grace without the cross, grace without Jesus Christ, living and incarnate.[8]

Unlike rules, discipleship is not simply about outward action. Rather, this entire book reminds us over and over again about how God can change us from the inside out. This is his work of grace in us. We only experience it when we give up living lives our own way. We find grace in freedom from our bondage to sin. We find grace in true fellowship with other believers. With a pastoral heart, Bonhoeffer insisted that, "We can only achieve perfect liberty and enjoy fellowship with Jesus when his command, his call to absolute discipleship, is appreciated *in its entirety*" (emphasis added).[9] The standards of discipleship first begin with inward transformation, and we receive this grace from Christ and through the work of the Holy Spirit that is active in a surrendered church and community of believers. As mentors, we simply hold up the standards of discipleship (*to know and love God, know our identity in Christ, and love our neighbors as ourselves*), and we lay out the cost of following Christ as we call others to live for something greater than themselves (1 John 5:3). This is not a lackluster pursuit. Regi Campbell articulates this understanding when he writes:

> Modern-day church people love classes, seminars, Bible studies, and small groups. We show up, sit in circles or rows, listen, share, pray, eat, and leave. Usually we do some homework in between meetings, but not too much (by design because we don't want to have fewer people involved by making it too hard). . . . We think that if we give homework, fewer people will show up. If we hold people accountable for doing the homework, we might embarrass them, and they won't come back. . . . We consistently compromise the quality of the program or of the learning experience in order to appease the peripheral participant.[10]

I agree with his diagnosis. And I say in response: "Stay on mission. Mentor on purpose. And don't compromise!" No loving parent grooms children with low expectations. No winning athlete approaches his training with low expectations. No good leader approaches work with low expectations.

It's a hard world that presses against the people of God in their homes, communities, schools, and churches. As mentors and disciple-makers, we want those we love to prepare for spiritual victory and to stand against the pull of the culture and the schemes of the Enemy. God calls us to make disciples, and we mentor on purpose because we want all of God's children to win.

Troop Welfare: It's Relational

Accomplishing the mission and winning the Christian race includes taking care of our troops relationally. Jesus spent his entire earthly ministry preparing his disciples to win. His teaching and training were not just about imparting knowledge and increasing learning (though it definitely included those things). His method of discipleship was relational.

Near the end of his life on earth, Jesus had an intimate exchange with his disciples. I imagine he spoke tenderly when he referred to them as friends in John 15:15–16. Although worthy, Jesus—who was both fully God and fully man—did not approach his disciples from a position of power, looking down at them from above. He became flesh and blood—a servant-leader—humbling himself. He engaged their suffering and reached out to his disciples as peers. He called them friends. Mentoring like our Savior means more than passing on knowledge; it means getting to know people by entering their worlds and investing in who they are. We must develop authentic, healthy relationships with those God has called us to mentor.

Troop welfare also includes self-leadership. Great mentors learn to become good stewards of their time so they can effectively invest in the lives of others. It's important to realize we can't invest in everyone we meet at the commitment level communicated in this book. Jesus was often surrounded by crowds of people. He healed and taught. He traveled a lot. He fixed family and political squabbles. He had religious debates and took time to play with children. He lived a full and productive life! But though he ministered to the masses, he invested deeply in the lives of only a select few. Even Jesus, the incarnate Son of God, did not try to fulfill the needs of every person he encountered. Jesus knew there would still be much work left to do, and he left that ministry to his disciples (John 14:12). As mentors, we need to accept both our ministry calling and our human limitations, realizing God is not asking us to meet the needs of others beyond our capacity. The beauty of mentoring and multiplying is we have the opportunity to train and equip others to respond in obedience, to share the load of ministry and make disciples. In this way, God's kingdom advances as he intends.

Practically, this means that we must be purposeful about how we use the time allotted us and exercise discernment regarding the relational investments we do make. Needs are all around us, some of which *could* be met and many we are probably passionate about, but discernment requires saying no at times. Good is often the enemy of great. Therefore, saying no to many *good* things can free you to say yes to the greater opportunities that are in direct alignment with the work God has uniquely assigned for you.

The *missio dei* or "mission of God" acknowledges that all ministry is important to the kingdom, and therefore we need the right people in the right places at the right times to commit to the work for which they are passionate, gifted, *and* called (1 Cor. 12). This is what it means to live our lives on purpose. The beauty of saying no to something that is good but not best at the moment is where we must trust God to fill the gaps. Ultimately, identified gaps provide wonderful training opportunities for mentees to contribute to God's kingdom work. We want those we mentor to understand their spiritual contributions and giftedness, to fearlessly walk in their callings, and to see how their obedience is beneficial to the overall work God is doing in their local church, community, and in the world.

The status quo in many churches is summarized by something called the 80/20 rule—where 20 percent of the people do 80 percent of the work. We need to reject this subpar standard. Not only is it unbiblical, it is a recipe for spiritual burnout of the faithful few. The goal of a mentoring ministry is not to burn out the willing and overlook the timid. We do not want disciples so consumed with doing an endless number of good deeds themselves that they are not making the commitment of being present with God, or submitting to the growth and transformation God desires for each of us to uniquely contribute to his kingdom. As we saw in the previous chapters, we are called to listen and be so in tune with God that we know what *our* unique kingdom contributions are (1 Cor. 12). By doing so, we faithfully practice mission accomplishment and troop welfare. We teach, train, and equip all disciples to contribute in their own unique ways to God's kingdom mission.

Mentor for Life

1. What kingdom work has God specifically called you to? Can you articulate the nature of that work? Write it down.

2. Have you ever thought about your faith as training? How has this chapter shaped the way you persevere on your faith journey?

3. How might you discipline yourself regarding the stewardship of work and time? What things might you need to stop doing? What training, preparation, or new experiences might you embrace?

4. As a mentor, what language will you use to communicate God's grace and kingdom mission to mentees? How can this understanding challenge the priorities of your life and theirs?

5. Mission Exercise: Read 1 Corinthians 12. Given the metaphor of the body of Christ, what "body part" do you represent? Write down how your role relates to that of other "parts" of the body. What people has God connected you with to complete his kingdom work? How do your passions, skills, and convictions work together to fulfill God's kingdom mission?

6. Summarize in four or five sentences what you have learned from this chapter.

Tweet This

"Christians who love Jesus and have made him
Lord over their lives live on purpose for God's
kingdom." #Mentor4Life @asistasjourney

Ten

Rally the Troops

It would be easy to become carried away in the pressure of reaching a goal to the point of neglecting the people involved, like an elephant stepping on an ant hill and destroying it without thinking of the absolute havoc wrought among the ants.

Dr. Carson Pue[1]

My daughter is a social butterfly with a bubbly personality. During a conference when she was in second grade, her teacher said, "I believe your daughter could make a friend out of a tree." I love that my girl is welcoming of others, yet sometimes her communication of that love and passion can be annoying. Last year, we went through a season when she continually talked about her "BFFs," or Best Friends Forever. She has matured quite a bit in one year, so we no longer hear that language. As a mother, however, I notice when she mentions some classmates' names more than others.

One day, I engaged her in conversation to ask about her friends. *What's cool about him? Why do you like her so much?* Concerning one friend in particular, she said, "When I was new to the school and didn't know anybody, she invited me in and introduced me to all of her friends." I nodded in approval and said, "That's a good quality to have in a friend. That's a great way to model Jesus." As I read the Gospels, I better understand that Jesus was all about inviting people of all backgrounds and walks of life into his kingdom. The fact that Jesus regularly invited children, Gentiles, women, sinners, the sick, and the poor—all groups considered socially undesirable—into his kingdom was a source of great contention among Jewish leaders. Subconsciously, we are prone to respond just like them and to reject the call of Jesus to make disciples of *all* people groups.

One way this partiality shows up is in the questions we ask. People have asked me many times, "What type of women do you have in the mentoring ministry?" It was initially difficult to formulate a response because somewhere under the surface of that question is another one, regarding who is in and who is out. I now believe the best answer is, "We are not looking for a certain 'type' of woman to commit to the mentoring ministry. By mentoring in small, diverse groups, we desire to create a safe place of belonging for everyone."

This question, however, does warrant serious consideration. If the purpose of mentoring as intentional discipleship is to focus on God and his kingdom mission, then we begin rightly when we first think about God and what he wants. We know what God wants because of what we read in his Word, and because of what Jesus commanded and practiced: we are commanded to make disciples of *all* people groups. Since we don't know whom God has called or convicted, we have a responsibility to reach out to everybody. You may recall that when we approach mentoring from the perspective of intentional discipleship, we are seeking to bridge the gap between our traditional practices of evangelism and a passive approach to discipleship. For this reason, we invite any woman who is interested in mentoring to join us on the journey of following Jesus.

This open invitation or rallying of the troops is for all. Word of mouth is the best marketing, not simply as a business practice, but also because it is relational. Personal invitations extended through relationships have allowed our ministry to grow tremendously. As a result of personal connections, we have all types of women involved in the mentoring ministry, including long-time church members,

members of other congregations, and even "unchurched" folks. Therefore, I encourage you to invite all women to participate, or to "rally the troops," because such is the will of God.

Who Will Come or Commit?

You may be thinking, "I am glad to invite anybody, but will they actually come?" While I understand and often share your concern, allow me to relieve your anxiety. You want people to commit to mentoring only when they are ready. Your responsibility is to remain open and prepared to respond. How you receive prospective mentees will largely depend on your thoughts concerning troop welfare and how well you actually know your troops. You must understand the troops—or in this case, the women you are reaching out to—before you can successfully rally them together for a specific cause.

For this reason, I must address the posture of the mentee for a moment. It is important for a mentor to understand that a mentee's willingness to show up is not the same as a commitment. Showing up would be like me arriving at the track meet or standing at the starting line of a race and maybe even getting into the starting blocks. If I don't start running when the track official fires his gun, however, I'm going nowhere. It is the same with someone's commitment to following Christ. A woman can say all the right things, utter a few prayers, and even show up for some events, but if her faith—however small—does not result in actions that get her moving in the right direction, that is a good indicator she is not ready or willing to commit to God, surrender to the work of the Holy Spirit, or learn from a mentor. A mentee must be willing to get moving and to take small steps.

Once we rally the troops and clearly communicate expectations, mentors must engage potential mentees concerning their willingness to actually commit to a mentoring group. We need to listen to their reasons for being interested because motivation is an important factor of consideration for troop welfare. Potential mentees may be tired of their current way of life and deeply desire change. Others understand they need Christ and that mentoring is a first step in growing as his disciple. Some will come simply because they are lonely and they want deeper friendships, or the mentoring opportunity may feel like their last hope. While drawing mentees nearer to Christ and setting them on his agenda is the primary mission, listening to the felt needs of your new mentees will help you serve them well. We care about the felt needs of the troops, and it's our responsibility as their mentors to connect their felt needs to the mission at hand.

Holy Tension: God's Mission and Our Felt Needs

Jesus understood these aspects of mission accomplishment and troop welfare. In fact, he constantly held two cares—his Father's will and the disciples' needs—in holy tension, and he never compromised on either of them. We must not forget that God has chosen to use people to accomplish his great work, so people are mission critical. Fallen people have real human needs that cannot be ignored, because it is difficult for any of us to stay focused on a mission if our felt needs are not met.

Troop welfare involves caring for people's bodies, minds, and souls.[2] Because our mentors are interested in drawing people in and becoming friends, we seek to care for the mentee's felt needs by ministering to the whole person. Peter Scazzero writes, "God made us as whole people, in his image (Gen. 1:27). That image includes physical, spiritual, emotional, intellectual, and social dimensions. . . . Ignoring any aspect of who we are as men and women made in God's image always results in destructive consequences—in our relationship with God, with others, and with ourselves."[3] While many church ministries are inviting and focus on meeting the spiritual needs of their members, few address the physical, emotional, intellectual, and social dimensions that make up the image bearer. Mentoring can fill this gap in some very practical ways.

While our mentoring ministry does not offer gym memberships, formal Christian counseling, or seminary classes, we do prepare our mentors to engage the important questions. We get real. One of my mentors regularly asks me, "When was the last time you and your husband had sex?" This is a woman who loves me and has an earnest desire to see my marriage thrive. I have often heard her say, "The church does a really good job of telling single people not to have sex, but a very poor job of encouraging married people to have sex all the time." Questions like this one, and my honest responses, provide a gateway into my physical, emotional, and social health and well-being. Sometimes I'll ask a woman, "How do you see God these days? How do you believe God sees you?" Her response to these questions gives me insight into her soul.

Asking hard questions can engage people and draw them in. This is a skill that can be learned, and it is very helpful for breaking down walls, especially in those areas where a person may be trying to push God away. Good mentors learn how to listen well, ask the right questions, and offer biblical perspective. We fail our sisters when we allow them to compartmentalize their lives. People bring their spiritual selves to church, take their work selves to the office, and drag their tired family selves back home. It's no wonder we walk around feeling defeated! We cannot focus on the "spiritual" self while neglecting the other elements that make us human. Mentoring speaks to the whole person, and it asks us to humbly journey with our troops into relationship. We don't outsource to strangers for help simply because it is the easiest thing to do.[4] We roll up our sleeves and enter into their messy lives.

As mentors, we rally the troops by asking hard questions. We listen well. We offer biblical counsel as appropriate. We experience life together. We deal with the spiritual without neglecting other important aspects of human life. Like Jesus, we see the needs of others and engage the questions they wrestle with when they are sick, downtrodden, and feeling unholy. In the midst of their struggles, Jesus offered his followers truth and hope. He said, "In this world you will have trouble. But take heart! I have overcome the world" (John 16:33). The incarnate Jesus entered our fallen world, and we follow his example when we share the same compassion, love, and hope that Jesus himself has offered us (2 Cor. 1:3–4).

Rallying Together for God's Mission

Jesus came to earth and was about his Father's business. People rallied around him because they were amazed by his devotion, teachings, and work. Not everybody who rallied followed, but Jesus was not distracted or manipulated by this. Likewise, as leaders, it is important that we are clear about our mission, and not distracted or manipulated to define success by the number of women who participate in our ministries. We miss the mark if our end state is simply to get people involved without making the long-term commitment to disciple them. Instead, birth your mentoring ministry out of a strong conviction to rally people and set them on a path to follow Jesus, to live their lives on purpose for God, and to join in the great work God is doing in the world. Through mentoring examples and with this book and its accompanying training resources, I want to equip and encourage you to prioritize discipleship.

Rally the troops by helping potential mentees see that they were created for a purpose and are part of something bigger than themselves. Don't settle for a ministry that gives people what they are used to, what they would personally prefer, or what makes them most comfortable. Those who want only a ministry that meets their personal needs or makes them feel better about life will most likely not commit to the expectations outlined here. Even if you start small, pray for those who long deeply for God, understand their need for change, and embrace a bigger, selfless purpose for life. In fact, sometimes it is best to start small. Isn't that how Jesus did it?

This Is How We Do It

Make the mentoring opportunity available to everybody. Share pertinent information and testimonies of transformation, and give potential mentees time to prayerfully ponder their decision.[5] Set clear and high expectations up front, and follow through.[6] Mentoring is a mutual commitment, and potential mentees should be clear about this commitment. Make yourself available to answer questions during their time of discernment. Give potential mentees the opportunity to speak with ministry leaders or other mentors to ask questions *before* they commit to a mentoring group.

After sharing the mentoring opportunity by word of mouth, we normally host an event to officially kick off the mentoring season. This is where mentees are given an opportunity to hear the vision of mentoring as intentional discipleship and commit to a mentoring group. Those who are interested complete an information form to communicate their availability. Afterward, someone from our leadership team reaches out within a few days to connect them with their mentors, who begin building relationships with them. All of this occurs prior to their first mentoring group gathering.

During the first group gathering, we ask everyone to sign a mentoring covenant that communicates the expectations and affirms their commitment to the group. The purpose of the covenant is to ensure that everyone understands and is committed to the same expectations and community goals. It is a tool for rallying the troops because it gives participants confidence in what to expect from their mentor and from each other, which in turn provides security. An alternative to the covenant might be writing down your group affirmations and reviewing them during your monthly gatherings.[7]

Your approach to mentoring and your processes will improve as you continue to mentor others. Part of that assessment will be regular communication with the mentoring leadership team and the mentees. We require all mentees to complete a feedback form at the end of each mentoring season. Without fail, we are reminded annually of the felt need for authentic relationships. (We will discuss the mentoring commitments of community and relationships more thoroughly in the following sections. For now, it is important to understand and communicate that a mentoring group is not a place where mentees will be rejected or abandoned.) Having authentic relationships is a felt need that cannot be ignored.

In reference to this relational concern, I found a Christianity Today *Leadership Journal* excerpt article titled "Why Small Groups Boom Then Bust" by Larry Osborne quite helpful. Pastor Osborne summarizes the history and challenges of small group ministry. Please note: I am careful to differentiate between a mentoring or discipleship ministry that utilizes a small group format (which I present in this book) and a typical small group ministry (which can be established for any number of reasons, and may or may not focus on discipleship).[8] In spite of this differentiation, I find Osborne's words ring true for the mentoring ministry as well. For example, he points out that a focus on division and multiplication within small group ministry can communicate the wrong values and priorities. He concluded that small group divisions reveal the following:

> Real relationships are considered disposable by those organizing the small group ministry. And that undercuts the purpose of the whole thing. A church's purpose for small groups and their people's reasons for attending must match for small groups to work. . . . I am convinced that the boom-and-bust

cycle of small groups could be easily stopped if those who lead small group ministries would simply remember why we started them in the first place and then ruthlessly stick to our original mission: helping people develop authentic and transparent Christian relationships.[9]

Unlike small group ministries, the primary mission of mentoring is not to help people "develop authentic and transparent Christian relationships." This is of course a complimentary by-product of mentoring and certainly addresses the felt need of mentees. The primary mission of mentoring is to make disciples who know and love God, know who they are in Christ, and love their neighbors. Because we believe making disciples is best accomplished by consistently and intentionally investing in fewer relationships over a longer period of time, we do not practice the "boom-and-bust" cycle. Unless it is absolutely necessary, we do not divide our mentoring groups.[10] With this understanding and these practices, we keep the primary mission in focus, while understanding the felt need of the troops to cultivate authentic relationships, and we affirm our value of mentoring and multiplying as mentioned in Chapter 4.

Mentoring groups gather once a month for a period of three hours.[11] Because people are used to meeting more frequently for small groups and Bible studies, they often ask, "How do mentors cultivate friendships within their mentoring group that go beyond the monthly gathering times?" The response to that question is totally up to the mentor. The monthly mentoring gathering is an intentional and structured gathering. It is the primary training ground for mentees. Mentors are encouraged, however, to exercise creativity and flexibility in addition to their monthly gatherings. Some mentors plan meals or complete community service or missions projects with their mentees. Others gather separately for Bible study. How you identify and respond to the felt needs of your mentees is totally up to you.

In summary: to rally the troops and balance the mission and felt needs, we intentionally keep mentoring groups small (approximately six mentees) and we ask for long-term relational commitments (one year). We commit our mentoring group gathering time to learning about God and participating in God's mission together. Stay focused on your mentoring mission: to teach and train women to know and love God, know who they are in Christ, and love their neighbors.[12] As you work to accomplish the mission, make sure you are also conscious and considerate of the felt needs of the troops. Cultivate God-centered relationships by prayerfully and intentionally calling people to follow Jesus. Love them well, and compassionately teach and equip them for works of service in God's kingdom. Focus on God's mission and rally the troops, because we want all of God's people prepared to run, fight, and win together!

Mentor for Life

1. How sensitive are you to the felt needs of others? Do people consider you a compassionate person? How do you know?

2. What are some of your felt needs? What characteristics do you look for in a friend? What are your expectations of a mentoring community? Are they realistic? Why or why not?

3. How can you create a healthy, mission-focused mentoring environment that is considerate of the felt needs of others?

4. As a mentor, how can you train yourself to ask questions that encourage self-reflection and growth? What are some tools and resources available to you?

5. Mission Exercise: The number one excuse I get for not mentoring or making disciples is, "I don't have time." Do you have time to mentor? One week has a total of 168 hours. Over the next seven days, document every hour of your activity.[13] At the end of the week, evaluate how your time was spent. Is this a normal weekly cycle or just an "off" week? Are you surprised by anything you see? Do you desire to make any changes? Take time to discuss this exercise and its findings with a trusted friend.

6. Summarize in four or five sentences what you have learned from this chapter.

Tweet This

"God has chosen to use people to accomplish his great work, so people are mission critical." #Mentor4Life @asistasjourney

Mentoring

A Commitment to Community

> *Many Christians think that having a personal*
> *relationship with God through Christ is all there is*
> *to Christianity. They are sorely mistaken, for there*
> *is that other dimension to the cross. The vertical*
> *trunk by itself does not make a cross. There is*
> *also the horizontal beam, appropriately called the*
> *crossbar. . . . The making of community cannot be a*
> *side issue or an optional matter for Christians. It is*
> *as important to God as one's individual salvation.*
> *Without community, there is no Christianity. Perfect*
> *community is to be found at the intersection of the two*
> *segments of the cross, where those who are reconciled*
> *with God can be reconciled together. Community is*
> *central to God's purpose for humankind.*
> *Gilbert Bilezikian[1]*

Committing to safe and trusting mentoring relationships
provides encouragement, accountability, and support.

Mentoring as intentional discipleship requires us to agree with
God that it is not good for humans to go through life isolated and alone.

Eleven

Be Your Sister's or Brother's Keeper

Sisterhood and brotherhood is a condition people have to work at.
Maya Angelou

Ring. Ring. Ring.

The phone rang, and I quickly picked it up.

"Hello, Captain Robinson. It's Midshipman London. Midshipman Houston is in trouble."[1]

I listened carefully as Midshipman London described the details of the previous day's events. She spoke of Midshipman Houston's lapse in judgment and her decision not to return to campus at the Naval Academy. I didn't know what to think. I had known both Midshipmen London and Houston since they were freshman college students; they were members of the gospel choir, a student worship community I had the privilege of serving as business manager. I was also a military officer at the time, which gave me the opportunity to mentor both of them for three years. They were the kind of midshipmen who would drop by my office unannounced to share their problems, ask questions, voice concerns, or get assistance with a project. We quickly developed a bond of accountability and support. I encouraged them, and they inspired me.

As Midshipman London shared her recollection of the events of the previous day, memories flooded my mind.

"Ma'am, she's not picking up the phone or returning anyone's phone calls, but I believe she will respond to you."

Grabbing a yellow sticky note, I jotted down Midshipman Houston's phone number and promised to call immediately. I hung up the phone, leaned back in my chair, and exhaled. *What in the world was she thinking?* It had been almost a year since my transition from the Naval Academy. Both girls were now seniors. Pulling a stunt like this could mean that Midshipman Houston would not graduate from the Naval Academy.

There was no point in contemplating the possible consequences of her decision now; the first course of action was getting her back to campus. The longer she stayed away, the harder it would be for her.

I made the call.

"Hello?"

Recognizing her voice on the other end of the line, I tried to be as casual as possible.

"Hey sweetie, this is Captain Robinson. How ya doin'?"

We talked for a while, and again several times over the next two days. I encouraged her to return to school and promised to be there to greet her when she arrived on campus. Thankfully, she made the right decision, and I arrived eager to give her a big hug. I knew the journey would not be easy, but I committed to be there through the correction process no matter the consequences. Over the next few months, she accepted responsibility for her actions, heeded correction, and eventually graduated. She was commissioned as a naval officer.

I sometimes wonder how things would have turned out if I had not received a call from Midshipman London that day, or if I had not called Midshipman Houston to challenge and encourage her to return to school. Both Midshipman London and I valued our mentoring relationship enough to do the difficult thing, and to love someone who was making a bad choice. As I think about this story, I'm reminded of the poignant question Cain asked God after killing his brother: "Am I my brother's keeper?" (Gen. 4:9). At the heart of Cain's sin was rage and jealousy, but even more problematic was Cain's distorted view of his relationship with God, which led to hatred of his brother. After the murder, the Lord asked Cain, "Where is your brother Abel?"(Gen. 4:9). Cain first responded with a lie—"I don't know"—and then had the audacity to answer God's question with a question of his own. Clearly, God already knew where Abel was and what Cain had done. By asking the question, God was calling Cain to give an account of his brother, and God was also clarifying that it was indeed Cain's responsibility to care about his brother's condition.

Cain's isolation, his rejection of God's standard, and the murder of his brother reminds us that we are not just responsible for our own lives. We go through this life together, and if we don't understand our desperate need for God or value his standards for our earthly relationships, we are sure to veer off on a wrong path. On the contrary, committing to a faith community that provides encouragement, accountability, and support makes us more compassionate people. In a safe and trusting mentoring community, love can overcome hate, and mercy can overcome passivity. Loving one another means we care about our sister's or brother's condition.

Being a Christian is not simply about my personal relationship with God through Christ. If it were, God would have taken me to heaven immediately upon my profession of faith. Being a Christian is really about whether I reject my own way and persevere in following Jesus daily. It is about graciously receiving the gift of the Holy Spirit, which empowers me to fulfill the Great Commandment to love God and love others. And being a Christian is about cultivating right relationships. Christianity is a relational faith—a vertical one regarding our relationship with God and a horizontal one involving our relationships with others. This is true from the beginning.

It Is Not Good for Anyone to Be Alone

We observe from Cain's choice that people who are not at peace sometimes take extreme measures like suicide or murder. At other times, they engage in shallow relationships or present the false positive sides of themselves to the world in an effort to gain the approval of others. It is not a healthy practice to respond "fine" or "okay" when someone genuinely asks me, "How are you doing?" Being my brother's or sister's keeper requires my willingness to ask and answer hard questions, and sometimes hear hard answers. We must go deeper in our relational commitments.

Presenting a false side of ourselves feeds into our human desire for attention and acceptance because we all want to feel loved. The use of technology and social media gives us an easy way to cry out for this attention or get a shallow sense of acceptance. It is so easy to "like" a beautiful selfie or make a positive comment while remaining isolated from true community or intimate face-to-face relationships. We are more socially connected today than ever, and yet many are increasingly concerned about the reality of our aloneness.2

God knows we need each other, and he knows we need him. I sometimes picture him looking down from heaven, observing all our shallow attempts to make ourselves attractive to others while he is crying out for us to draw near to him. I imagine him asking us the same question he asked Cain, "If you do what is right, will you not be accepted?" (Gen. 4:7). There is no doubt our personal relationship with God is important for our Christian faith and our salvation. Yet because of God's concern for *all* humanity, he asks us, "Where is your brother?" or "Where is your sister?" In so many ways, we selfishly follow the sinful response of Cain by asking God, "Am I my brother's keeper?"

By now, we understand that the answer to that question is, "Yes, I am my sister's keeper." This acceptance includes the humble reality that sharing the same concern God has for other people can be a challenge. It is humbling when people perform better than us. Our temptation might be to respond in jealousy like Cain. It can make us angry or prideful when people don't do the right thing. The temptation may be to reject or judge them. Like Midshipman Houston, people generally know when they mess up. They don't always need us to remind them of that. The loving and sacrificial work of mentoring means journeying with a mentee through her mess so she doesn't feel alone and abandoned by God or her community.

I love to see the art community at work, because good art reflects the glory of God. Artist Gilbert Young has a piece called "He Ain't Heavy." It's a simple image of a man reaching up his arm to connect with another stronger man who is reaching down over a concrete wall to lift him up. This is a great picture to me of what a mentor does. Sometimes, we may not want to be our sister's keeper. We may not want to mentor because we feel like the work is too hard or the load is too heavy. But in his grace, God continues to reach down to us. And as we learn to reach up to him, we find we are also able to reach down and grab hold of our sisters with the humble reminder God gives us: "She ain't heavy." This is a picture of what it looks like to commit to a safe and trusting mentoring community.

In *FullFill* magazine, Anita Lustrea[3] concluded that we all have a need for community.[4] The results of an online survey of over 2,300 women confirmed the need for intimate relationships as one of the top three recurring macro themes. In the column, Anita shared some of the fears we have when cultivating relationships, and discussed the health benefits that can result from having friendships. Gleaning from Dr. Cloud and Dr. Townsend, she also described the types of friends we all need. For example, we all need to find safe people we can trust. In their book *Safe People*, Dr. Henry Cloud and Dr. John Townsend conclude that safe people have three characteristics: 1) they draw us closer to God, 2) they draw us closer to others, and 3) they draw us closer to our authentic selves.[5] In mentoring groups, we want to create safe communities, which begins with our compassionate commitment to become our sisters' keepers. God loves us, and he calls us out of isolation and into safe communities so we do not take extreme measures like murder or suicide, and so we can receive help when our lives are a mess.

We all need help at one point or another from real friends who aid us in responding to life's challenges rightly, boldly, and courageously. Safety and trust are the foundations of any healthy friendship. Sometimes, we know what we *ought* to do, we just need the proper support to get from here to there. This is true for anyone who is lost, who is without hope, or who lacks faith. It's true of young believers learning how to follow Christ. It's true for someone who is suffering or struggling with questions about God. It's also true for anyone going through a transition or someone who is not sure where to turn or what to do next. At various points in life, we all feel unsure, devalued, or out of place. Stop and think for a moment: *Who in your life do you trust to give you wise counsel? Thank God right now for the willing hearts who graciously offer help when we need it.* This is the reason God calls us into safe and trusting communities where we can grow in our dependence on him, understand our identity, and hear him affirm, "You are not alone."

In safe and trusting communities, we find our purpose. We blossom and become the women God designed for his glory. Janet O. Hagberg and Robert A. Guelich write:

> Becoming more and more who God designed you to be means becoming progressively more humble and dependent on God. You know you are set apart to do the unique work God calls you to do, yet it might initially make you feel isolated from some of the people you used to spend time with.

But something becomes possible if you accept this tension: true community. Biblical community is the unity in diversity of people who embrace their own and each other's uniqueness, becoming God's arms, feet, and hands on earth. We don't always understand each other, but that's all right because we share what it means to be faithful to God in living out our distinctive individuality together—maintaining unity through the Holy Spirit.[6]

God desires for us to live out our faith together in community, and if we are willing to take the risk of committing to mentoring relationships, he has divinely appointed safe people who are trustworthy to connect with us. Do not fear. There is no reason to journey through life alone. A mentor from my ministry shares her testimony:

Why do I continue to be amazed at all the things God does rather than expecting he will do them? The mentoring ministry is just another example of amazement. It's hard for me to believe that our group has bonded so well in such a short period of time. During our recent mentoring gathering, one mentee remarked that she thought God had put together the perfect group for her, and we all agreed.

Each for the Other

Contrary to our western values and practices of individualism and pulling ourselves up by our own bootstraps, God is intently interested on working in the hearts of individuals so he can use them to change communities. God told Adam and Eve to be fruitful and multiply the earth. He called Abraham so through him all nations would receive God's blessing. He used Moses and Joshua to bring his chosen people out of slavery and into the Promised Land. God sent his son, Jesus, so salvation can be made available in his new kingdom, and so those who believe in him will be saved. Peter preached the good news of this kingdom with boldness, and thousands were able to enter into it. Paul was given the specific task of ministering and taking the good news of this kingdom to the Gentiles. From the beginning of the Bible until the end, God is interested in getting all humankind back on track with his original plan of oneness with him, oneness with each other, and oneness with creation.

By every human standard, these "keepers" of God's vision were ordinary people who were confronted with their desperate need for God. Once they made the decision to commit to his mission, they responded in obedience and were able to positively impact the lives of others. All of them were groomed and refined in community. Prior to their sin, Eve and Adam were on mission for God together to act as custodians of a beautiful garden and everything in it. Abraham left his family of origin and set out on a journey to the land God showed him with his wife, Sarah. As his family increased and circumstances changed, Abraham grew in his faith. Moses partnered with Miriam and Aaron[7] to lead the Israelites out of slavery in Egypt. After being mentored by and warring[8] alongside Moses, Joshua led the Israelites into the land God promised them. Joshua stood in obedience with the priesthood of God to serve the people of God. Throughout his earthly ministry, Jesus consistently traveled with his twelve disciples and a group of women. In the New Testament epistles, we are made aware of the many women and men who worked alongside Paul to ensure God's mission to share the gospel with the Gentiles was fulfilled. None of these keepers of God's mission traveled through life alone.

Additionally, many of them gave up their earthly desires so they could obey the call of God on their lives. As the oldest son in a patriarchal society, it would have been right for Abraham to remain with his family of origin, take up his father's trade, and receive all the blessings of the first son.[9] Abraham gave that up because he understood his desperate need for God. As the adopted son of Pharaoh's daughter, Moses could have continued to enjoy the pleasures of the palace and the priesthood in his adult life. He saw the oppression of his people, however, which ignited his desire for justice. He gave up his life of privilege because he understood his desperate need for God. Jesus understood the mission that was set before him. He had no real place to call "home" on this earth and gave up his life because of his desperate desire to fulfill God's will. Prior to his conversion, Paul was a man of status and privilege. Because he was sold out to God's mission, he became a traveling evangelist and church planter. He even forsook marriage and worked to earn his own salary in some cases so he could attend to the Lord's work without distraction and not be a financial burden to others.[10] God changed Paul's desires, which led to the Gentiles receiving good news. Paul gave up his former understanding of what was right because he understood his desperate need for God.

God wants to shape our earthly desires into his likeness. He often does this by providing a safe and trusting community that gives us encouragement, accountability, and support. Our purpose is clarified when we commit to others who will partner with us on our faith journeys. It is in the essence of our work—in a diverse community with other believers who are also on mission for God—that we are shaped and strengthened to continue pursuing Jesus.

Submitting to others in an interdependent community can be humbling. Humility is what leads us to an "others-centered" life. To this end, Paul wrote that we should imitate Christ: "Do nothing out of selfish ambition or vain conceit. Rather, in humility value others above yourselves, not looking to your own interests but each of you to the interests of the others" (Phil. 2:3–4). We are our sisters' keepers, and when we commit to mentoring, we turn away from ourselves—first, upward toward God, and second, out-ward toward other people. This turning away is how we learn to prioritize God's mission, lay down our individual desires, humble ourselves, and submit to each other out of reverence for Christ. That's the value of mentoring in a small community.

Mentor for Life

1. What does it practically look like for you to live an others-focused life?

2. Do you know someone right now who needs the reminder that God has not forgotten them and they are not alone in this world? What special way can you reach out to that person this week?

3. At times, the responsibility of mentoring can feel heavy. What are some ways you can rejuvenate or encourage yourself when mentoring seems too hard?

4. How can understanding the needs of others, God's mission, and even your own wants and desires (good or bad) better equip you to mentor authentically in a safe community?

5. Community Exercise: Consider hosting a dinner party this month for four women you know but have never invited to dinner. Pray for these women as you prepare to serve them. Make the evening an informal and relational time. Plan for an intentional time of eating and focused table talk.[11]

6. Summarize in four or five sentences what you have learned from this chapter.

Tweet This

"Mentors walk through life's messes so their mentees don't feel alone and abandoned by God or their community." #Mentor4Life @asistasjourney

Twelve

This Makes a Family

It takes a whole village to raise a child.
African Proverb

Growing up, I lived in close proximity to my extended family. I could take a quick walk to several of their homes, and those who lived farther were just a short car ride away. As a child, I loved spending quality time with my family. The weekends presented opportunities for play and fun. Holidays were big family events filled with lots of food and adult drama. I miss some of those special moments. Even though those gatherings brought an assurance of tension or some confrontation, we loved each other and were bonded for life. Being in a family gave us a sense of belonging.

As humans, we all desire to belong—to be part of something bigger than ourselves. Indeed, we are created for community. As members of a community, we all have a responsibility to cultivate the village, and that commitment is what actually makes a real community. My extended family and their neighbors understood the African proverb, "It takes a whole village to raise a child," and thus my safe and loving community was bigger than my immediate, biological family. It included the voices of teachers, coaches, mentors, community leaders, and neighbors, who all spoke into my life with equal authority. If a neighbor found me doing something disrespectful, discipline was immediate. Only later would they tell my parents. If the incident was severe enough, it's likely my parents would give me another consequence when I returned home—both for being disrespectful of my elders and for making them look bad in public. Parents, family members, community leaders, and churchgoers loved me enough to pay attention to my behavior and to set boundaries for my protection. Boundaries are for our benefit. Boundaries made me feel safe as a child. Because of my community's discipline and loving instruction, I knew without a shadow of doubt who really cared about me and my future. In this nurturing mentoring community, I received encouragement, accountability, and support.

Identification Markers: Belonging to God's Family

Unfortunately, not everyone is raised in a safe, loving, and disciplined environment. Some people grew up in families that were not safe or trusting, and therefore, they do not trust others. It is easy to yield to the temptation to isolate ourselves when we have been disappointed by people, but even within the flaws of our biological families, Christ gives us hope. Our biological families are where we began our life on earth; however, they do not determine where we end up or how we choose to live as responsible adults. On the contrary, when we become Christians, God connects us with a new spiritual family, a family that affirms the finished work of Christ on the cross, affirms our true identity in him, and yields to the power of the Holy Spirit to change hearts and transform lives. Our spiritual family helps us find our purpose in God's master plan.

When Jesus began his earthly ministry, his biological family did not understand his purpose or calling. As a matter of fact, they thought he was crazy.[1] Jesus understood that his commitment to his heavenly Father required a detachment from his earthly family, particularly if his biological family was not living for God's purposes. Jesus pointed to his disciples and said, "Here are my mother and my brothers. For whoever does the will of my Father in heaven is my brother and sister and mother" (Matt. 12:49–50). Committing to a mentoring community provides the encouragement, accountability, and support needed to do the will of our heavenly Father.

As mentors, we extend open arms as the body of Christ to all the children of God's family. Our true brothers and sisters are those who do the will of our heavenly Father. Once sons and daughters are brought into the fold, it is important to distinguish the family markings—those characteristics that make us unique from people in the world who do not belong to God.

What sets Christians apart from others? What are our distinguishable characteristics? When people see us, how do they know we belong to God's family?

The Bible is pretty clear that the primary distinguishing mark of God's children is love. Therefore, above all else, mentors must teach and model how to love God and others well.

Love is more than just a feeling or physical attraction. The Greek language has four words that define different forms of love.[2] The word *agape* best communicates the unconditional love or Christian love as defined and practiced in the New Testament. *Agape* brings us together in Christian community through acts of compassion, forgiveness, and generosity. *Agape* also affirms our commitment to God. Twice in the gospel of John, Jesus confirms that the commitment to love is intricately connected to *our faithful obedience to God.*[3] Love is observable in the choices we make and the way we live and act toward others. Committing to love is an affirmation of our ability to trust and be trusted. As sisters in Christ, we understand that trust is a choice to offer ourselves as people who are worthy of trust (1 Tim. 6:20). Trust is also a choice we make to act and respond in love (1 Cor. 13:6–7).

Committing to love is also an affirmation of our trust in God. Our love compels us to obedience when we trust that God's plan for our lives is better than pursuing our own way. Jesus closes the Great Commission passage of Matthew 28:19–20 by charging the disciples to teach his followers to *obey* everything he commands. Our love of God is intricately connected to our obedience to God, and serves as an indicator that we are indeed children in God's family.

I have heard all kinds of justifications for Christians not responding as a family to provide healthy boundaries that nurture our spiritual growth. Ultimately, we don't want to do the hard things, and yet we don't want to answer to charges of being unloving, self-righteous, or judgmental. Our fears prevent us from responding in faith and from providing loving correction or a gentle rebuke when a sister or brother is not obeying the Lord. Sin is not simply defined as the bad things we do—missing the mark or disobeying God's commands. Sin also includes the good things we neglect or fail to do. The apostle James wrote, "If anyone, then, knows the good they ought to do and doesn't do it, it is sin for them" (James 4:17). He closes his letter by admonishing his brothers, "If one of you should wander from the truth and someone should bring that person back, remember this: Whoever turns a sinner from the error of their way will save them from death and cover over a multitude of sins" (James 5:19–20). I assure you, there is nothing more unloving than ignoring sin and allowing a sister or brother to continue on a path of disobedience toward God.

Remember

Remembering who we are and what God has done is another important practice we engage in as members of God's family. Its foundations are found in the Old Testament. In his last instructions to the Israelites, Moses highlights the importance of this practice on several occasions:

What other nation is so great as to have their gods near them
the way the LORD our God is near us whenever we pray to
him? And what other nation is so great as to have such righteous decrees and laws as this body of laws I am setting before
you today? Only be careful, and watch yourselves closely so
that you do not forget the things your eyes have seen or let
them fade from your heart as long as you live. Teach them to
your children and to their children after them. (Deut 4:7–9)

Hear, O Israel: The LORD our God, the LORD is one. Love
the LORD your God with all your heart and with all your soul
and with all your strength. These commandments that I give
you today are to be on your hearts. Impress them on your
children. Talk about them when you sit at home and when
you walk along the road, when you lie down and when you
get up . . . be careful that you do not forget the LORD. (Deut.
6:4–7, 12)

And now, Israel, what does the LORD your God ask of
you but to fear the LORD your God, to walk in obedience
to him, to love him, to serve the LORD your God with all
your heart and with all your soul, and to observe the LORD's
commands and decrees that I am giving you today for your
own good? . . . the LORD set his affection on your ancestors
and loved them, and he chose you, their descendants, above all
the nations—as it is today. Circumcise your hearts, therefore,
and do not be stiff-necked any longer (Deut 10:12–13, 15–16).

The act of remembrance lets us know we are not alone in this
world. God is present with us. When we remember God's presence, we better understand the history of our Christian family
and heritage. We affirm our true identity and commitment to this
family every time we read the Word of God to learn history from
the patriarchs, prophets, kings, priests, and apostles; every time we
cry out to Yahweh through prayers or songs of deliverance; every
time we read a Christian biography or study the life of a hero or

"shero" of the faith; and every time we praise and listen intently to a testimony shared in our midst.

Remembering is an act of discipline. As mentors, remembering gives us the opportunity to remind God's children of who he is and what he has done. Remembering also reminds us of who we are in him. In the same way I can look back and recall the names, faces, and memories of all those villagers who have greatly enriched my life, God's children need to know and remember the life stories of those in their spiritual family. This includes people of faith in the Bible, Christians throughout church history, and the stories of those in their immediate church family. This type of remembrance is part of the makings of a family and must be celebrated in Christian community.

Affirming God's Family in Community

Sometime after I entered the military, I realized not everyone had the same support and encouraging "village" experiences I had growing up. Some people enter the military because they have never experienced a safe community. They are looking for a place to belong, or at least a way to escape their biological circumstances. Although wonderful bonds are formed through military training and serving together, unfortunately, they can be short-lived because military personnel move so frequently and are stationed all over the world. For service members, life sometimes feels like an endless series of breakups. We enter into intimate relationships, and then we are physically separated by a mandatory move or deployment from those we love.

This is true, not just of the military, but of many relationships in our culture today. It is increasingly rare to find people who are born, raised, and then remain their entire lives in the same community. Some go off to college or enter the military. Changes in marital relationships and jobs cause us to uproot families all the time, and wherever people move, they need a place to connect. When people feel disconnected or don't have a sense of belonging, their relational deficiencies present huge challenges. These challenges include the lack of a safe and trusting community that leaves them without encouragement, accountability, or support. We all need a family, a place, or a community that feels like home.

One helpful way of thinking about relational needs is the model presented by Robert J. Wicks in his book, *Touching the Holy: Ordinariness, Self-Esteem, and Friendship.* Wicks documents the types of friends or "voices" we all need in our lives. The first voice is that of the "prophet." The prophet presents the strong voice of a person who is "living an honest and courageous life guided by truth and compassion."[4] The prophet speaks God's truth into our lives by challenging us to confront and deal with issues in a manner pleasing to the Lord.

In addition to the prophet, we also need a "cheerleader." This person is sometimes needed to "balance the prophetic voices."[5] The cheerleader helps us see ourselves through the eyes of our loving Abba, Father God. The cheerleader reminds us that we are sons and daughters of the King who loves us and has a good plan and purpose for our lives. A cheerleader is *not* an enabler, someone to abuse, or simply someone to help us feel better about ourselves or our sin; rather, a cheerleader supports us on our spiritual journey.[6]

The third voice Wicks presents is that of the "harasser." This is a person who will not allow us to take ourselves too seriously as we grow in our relationship with God. The harasser is the "type of friend [who] helps us regain and maintain perspective (so we don't unnecessarily waste valuable energy)."[7] The word *harass* often carries a negative connotation, which I think distracts from the main point Wicks is trying to make in his friendship paradigm. Unlike the prophet who speaks truth, or the cheerleader who encourages, the harasser in our lives is often the person who serves by speaking in some ways like a conscience. She is the accountability partner—the person who reminds us of who we are when we doubt ourselves. She helps us not to lose heart on the journey by encouraging rest, soul care, and fun. "The prophet enhances our sense of single-heartedness. The cheerleader generously showers us with support we feel we need. The harasser encourages us to maintain a sense of proper perspective."[8]

Wicks completes his friendship paradigm with a group of voices that are particularly helpful for spiritual growth. He writes that the fourth group of voices we all need in our lives is that of spiritual guides. These are people and resources (books, blogs, and so on) that can "help us deal with our unrecognized and unnecessary fears . . . help us to appreciate the need for proper detachment, and . . . lead us to a sense of enthusiasm and perspective in a world strained by anxiety and confusion."[9] Spiritual guides include our mentors, of course. They also include:

- Spiritual companions, or "people who call us to be all that we can be without embarrassing us because we are presently where we are,"[10]
- Spiritual mothers and fathers, or wise people we seek out for help at crucial moments in our lives, and
- Books and places (or your mentoring resources) that help us see God clearly and meet with him without distraction.[11]

Thank God for our true friends and family. These relationships are shaped through love, trust, and obedience. Our Christian heritage and identity are affirmed through remembering God's story and his work throughout history. God has not left us alone in this world. He is present with us, and we have each other. Providing a Christian family is God's way of fulfilling our need for the sense of belonging. Within this family and community, God uses a variety of "voices" or friendships to shape us. That's the benefit of mentoring within the context of a small group. Through mentoring, we value these diverse contributions and "voices" as gifts from God, and commit to cultivating our new family with each of them.

This Is How We Do It

What does the making of a Christian family look like in real life? As previously mentioned, I believe mentoring is best done in the context of small groups of no more than six mentees. This is because, unlike a one-on-one mentoring relationship, a mentoring group invites us into a diverse community and increases the likelihood that we will have several "voices" available to complement each other and speak into our lives. Intentionally diversifying mentoring groups also increases the chance of finding a spiritually and emotionally balanced community where trust and accountability provide safe boundaries for all involved.

A mentoring community must also place a high value on guarding the gift of sound Bible teaching and the gift of fellowship among believers. I guard the gift of sound teaching by having all mentors on the leadership team read all selected mentoring resources prior to the start of each mentoring season. Together, the mentoring leaders discern and affirm the best resources to share with mentees that season. All mentoring groups then go through the same mentoring resource material. In this way, all mentees are receiving the same instruction, and a healthy boundary is in place.

Guarding the gift of fellowship means we offer ourselves to others as people of character, and as safe and trustworthy people. We accept the responsibility of being our sister's keeper, present our authentic selves, and share freely but appropriately to increase intimacy within the mentoring group. We are helpful. We are not judgmental. We do not gossip. We do not repeat what is shared in the mentoring group with others outside the group.[12] We engage and respond as sisters in Christ who desire to draw closer to God, conform to his image, and draw closer to each other.[13]

We also make the choice to trust others. Choosing to trust is an act of love. First Corinthians 13:6–7 reads, "Love does not delight in evil but rejoices with the truth. It always protects, always trusts, always hopes, always perseveres." Often, we are unwilling to present our true selves out of fear of what others will say or how we will be received. But fear is not a Christ-centered motivation. It is not helpful for our personal growth or for the intimacy we desire to have with others. If my husband asks me, "How are you doing?" and I respond with a quick-tempered, "Fine," he looks me in the eye and says, "That tells me you are not fine." What my initial response really communicates is, "I don't know how I'm doing and may need some help with that," or "I know exactly how I am doing, but I don't want to talk about it right now." Either way, the truth is that I *do* need help and I *do* need him. In the same manner, committing to a mentoring community requires us to commit to trusting others even when we are uncertain about our own feelings.

Love always protects, trusts, hopes, and perseveres. Loving others as God intends is something we practice together in a safe and trusting mentoring community. For that reason, we can learn to trust others with our needs and ask, expect, and even teach others how to love us well. Dr. Cloud and Dr. Townsend remind us that learning to *ask* for love is important:

1. When we ask, we develop humility.
2. When we ask, we are owning our needs.
3. When we ask, we are taking initiative.
4. When we ask, we are developing a grateful character.
5. Asking increases the odds that we'll get something.[14]

We must learn to ask for love, to embrace our spiritual family, and to create safe communities. By committing to community, we present ourselves as trustworthy people and people who are willing to trust others. This is how we become our sister's keeper, and this is how true love abounds.

Mentor for Life

1. How do you know when you are loving or being loved well?

2. What prevents you from trusting others?

3. To mentor effectively, you must confront and answer the question: Am I a trustworthy person? Have you developed habits of gossiping, judging, inappropriately sharing information, or criticizing others? Ask some of your closest friends to share their honest perceptions concerning your trustworthiness.

4. To mentor effectively, you must also confront and answer the question: Am I a safe person? Do you have a habit of hurting other people? Have you maintained healthy, long-term relationships in your adult life? Are you helpful? How do you respond when others are rejoicing or mourning? Again, take some time to reflect on your own relationship and patterns to determine if any unhealthy habits need addressing before leading a mentoring relationship.

5. Community Exercise: Make a list of the safe and trustworthy people in your life. Sit down and write each of them a thank-you card this month, specifically communicating the ways they have modeled safety and trust in your life and how those actions have shaped your understanding of being part of God's family.

6. Summarize in four or five sentences what you have learned from this chapter.

Tweet This

On Community: "Safe communities consist of trustworthy people and people who are willing to trust others." #Mentor4Life @asistasjourney

Mentoring

A Commitment to Relationships

> *Jesus offended people by what he said, as well as by what he did. He touched, ate, healed, named, loved, celebrated, listened, served and died for all the wrong people. Jesus acted. And that was a problem. . . . This act of paying attention is the core of our discipleship, proof of our worship and evidence that our shuttered windows are now open and opening wider still.*
>
> *Mark Labberton*[1]

A relational commitment to mentoring requires that we embrace people as God does and welcome diverse relationships that reflect true unity in the body of Christ.

Mentoring as intentional discipleship requires a compassionate embrace of God's invitation and message for *all* women.

Thirteen

Embrace Unity in Diversity

The church is known for her diversity, her ability to embrace every single person.

Darlene Zschech[1]

The first time I stepped onto her porch, it was a sweltering hot summer day in Maryland. I'd been encouraged to visit the woman who lived in this house because she was offering a Bible study for young women, and that's exactly what I needed. Although I'd been raised in the church, I was really just a young Christian at the time—only a year into a personal relationship with the Lord. I was still unsure about a lot of things, including what it even meant to be a disciple. I wanted to learn.

The door opened, and Mary stepped into my life with her smile, warm hugs, homemade bread, and Snickers cookies. But she didn't stop there. She shared the Word of God and taught me his truth. It was Mary who prayed me through some of the most difficult times in my young adult life. It was Mary who became one of my closest confidants and advisors. It was Mary who corrected my many shortcomings.

Mary was the first woman who intentionally discipled me. As a young midshipman from South Carolina attending the United States Naval Academy, I didn't know how to cook. I rarely washed my own clothes. Aside from keeping a clean house, being hospitable, and throwing a great party, I knew little about homemaking because my mother proudly took care of those things. Her priority was to ensure that we, her children, had every opportunity to prepare academically and athletically for our futures. And while personal leadership, responsibility, and accountability were ingrained in me at a young age, I never learned certain life lessons as a child.

Mary gained wisdom from persevering through life. She was an older white woman, a former nurse, a devoted wife, and a stay-at-home mom. This mother of five (four of whom were still living at home) regularly taught women's Bible studies, homeschooled her children, and was devoted to serving midshipmen, her church, and her community. She baked the best treats from scratch. During my visits, she would cook and I would eat. I was quite pleased with this arrangement. We were very different, and God used our differences to create opportunities for learning and to grow a beautiful relationship.

We didn't define our friendship. Exactly what words do you use to define an uncommon yet intimate relationship that crosses generational, racial, and cultural lines? Because I didn't have the right language, I had difficulty explaining our relationship to other people. Mary wasn't a biological family member, nor was she my godmother or a surrogate parent. I would say things like, "She's my spiritual advisor" (which surely gave the image of a false prophet with a crystal ball) or "She's my spiritual director" (an unfamiliar term at the time, but which has now become a well-known term). It never occurred to me to say, "She is discipling me." That language was not commonly used in my church context.

Our college environment had an organic leadership component that included mentoring, but I never thought to use the word *mentor* to define my relationship with Mary. In hindsight, I see this as one of the problems with compartmentalizing our lives. In my mind, mentoring was something that happened professionally. I fully expected military officers to teach and train me, to point me in the right direction. Mary was doing the same kind of work, but because she was operating in the "spiritual part" of my life, the label "mentor" did not come to mind. Mentoring was the true nature of our relationship, however, and for that I will be eternally grateful.

Mary and I had many personality differences, but we continued in our relationship by embracing unity or oneness in our diversity. Because we were both a part of God's family, we took the risk and confronted our fears. We asked each other difficult questions and did not shy away from conflict. We didn't try to pretend that we were blind to "color"[2] or that our racial or ethnic heritage did not influence the way we read Scripture, voted, or viewed the world. We weren't afraid to share our emotional baggage and how our different social and economic experiences shaped us. We were different, and that was okay. In fact, it was good and necessary for our growth and for our service to the church. Because we were willing to push through our areas of discomfort in spite of our differences, God stretched us individually, and we are both better as a result. Mary changed the way I saw the world, and I influenced the way she viewed others who did not share her same experiences.

Mentoring across racial, ethic, generational, and socioeconomic lines influences the way we experience God and love others. Through mentoring, we make relationship commitments that require us to embrace people as God does and welcome diverse relationships that reflect true unity in the body of Christ. When we learn to love those who are different from us, we begin to see beyond ourselves and through the eyes of Jesus instead. In his book, *The Dangerous Act of Loving Your Neighbor*, Mark Labberton writes:

> Seeing is important and reliable in many ways, but it is neither neutral nor comprehensive. Sight is not just what we see but how we see—and that is the function of values, experiences, relationships, associations, beliefs, culture, race, gender and age. This means that everything we see passes

through invisible lenses of perception that take a lot of the information the eye receives and the brain sorts, and place it within the framework of our experience or understanding or plausibility. . . . Spoken or unspoken, our sight filters instantly allow some information in and keep some out, categorizing, framing, typing. They prioritize what we are attracted to and barely register what we find irrelevant. We move seamlessly from sight to perception, from the information available to the assignment of value and meaning to what we see. We don't see ourselves perceiving. We just see. This means we can be blind about our seeing. Just as sight is not neutral, it is not comprehensive. That is, physical sight goes only so far; it does not include what is invisible. . . . So, beyond the typical range of limitations is the fact that we cannot see or know someone else's heart. That is the fundamental and profound limitation in our sight.[3]

God values diversity in our relationships because it helps us acknowledge our own blindness and our tendency to misperceive or wrongly judge the motivations of others. As we grow in relationships with those who are different from us, we begin to clean off our eyeglasses and enter their life experiences with compassion. Our sight improves. We cannot wholeheartedly or effectively make disciples of all nations and fulfill the Great Commission if we have limited scope and poor vision that prevent us from loving our neighbor across town or down the street. In her book, *Disunity in Christ: Uncovering the Hidden Forces That Keep Us Apart*, reconciler and social psychologist Dr. Christena Cleveland writes, "To respond to God's call fully, we need to express our interdependent diversity in individual churches, denominations and organizations as well as in the worldwide body of Christ."[4] Mentoring through diverse relationships helps us live as people of integrity in light of the gospel we proclaim.

See This: We Are All Different by Design

Seeing people as God sees them means we acknowledge our differences and embrace the diversity within the body of Christ as a gift from God. In his book about marriage, *What Did You Expect?* Dr. Paul David Tripp talks about the need for a husband and wife to acknowledge their differences as the good intention and created purpose of God. Only by accepting and valuing their differences can they have a healthy marriage and thrive together. He writes:

> Everything that makes up [your spouse] . . . came out of the mind of an incredibly creative designer. . . . [The designer, God] was not locked into one model of what a human being is. . . . [5] It is hurtful to your spouse when you disrespect her for things she did not choose or reject her for things she cannot change. Every difference [in personality, strengths or weaknesses, gifts, talents, passions, and so on] is an opportunity to celebrate God's creative artistry and a chance to communicate specific respect and appreciation for who God has formed your spouse to be.[6]

Dr. Tripp wants the reader to see that any rejection of the unique differences in a spouse is not only a rejection of the spouse, but is also a rejection of the God who created the spouse. Wow! I know this truth was convicting upon my first reading. It forced me to reevaluate the way I viewed my spouse, who has a personality different from mine. As a result of valuing our differences, I better appreciate our specific contributions as God's gifts to each other, and as necessary to his purpose in forming us through our marriage.

186 The Mentoring Commitment

The Beauty of Embrace

Learning to embrace our differences and welcome diverse relationships into our lives is important for our spiritual formation. People who are different will make us uncomfortable and challenge us. This is cause for humility. Hopefully, these encounters will help us listen better, see more clearly, and become more compassionate. Compassion is necessary for a follower of Jesus, especially when we consider Jesus' actions on behalf of the marginalized, undervalued, sinners, and social outcasts of his day. I've given much thought to the mentor's need for compassion particularly when I consider the rejection some people experience in the body of Christ. Hurt and broken women are aimlessly walking around our sanctuaries or avoiding the church altogether because intuitively, we all know when we do not fit the mold and when we are not wanted.[77]

God calls us to lovingly embrace others regardless of our differences. God purposely made each of us—male and female, young and old, Jew and Gentile, slave and free—beautifully different. While our differences may challenge us, they are also a means of the transformative work God wants to do in each of our hearts, both individually and within Christian community. God uses our differences to mold us as we seek to love unconditionally and develop God-honoring relationships with all people who are made in the image of God.

My mentor, Mary, and I are still two very different people. If you would have placed us in a room together with other strangers prior to the establishment of our relationship, we probably wouldn't have naturally gravitated toward each other. That's not necessarily a bad thing. In fact, it's normal for us to desire connections with people who either look like us or make us feel most comfortable because those places shape and affirm our cultural identity. We like being with people who share our common interests, experiences, work, or family configurations.

But when we connect *only* with people with whom we have something in common, we miss out on wonderful opportunities to nurture other relationships God can use to transform us into the likeness of Christ, and to fulfill the Great Commission. We cannot go into the world and share the gospel with a pure heart if we are unwilling to do that same work and cultivate those same relationships across town or down the street. We are all a part of a new family, remember? Dr. Cleveland writes:

> Our commitment to the other members of the body of Christ should trump our desire [to be comfortable only with those who are just like us]. . . . Our submission to God, irrevocable commitment to each other and interdependence should hold us together when we want to distance ourselves from Christians who fail to live up to our gold standards or who complicate our lives.[8]

A full embrace of Christ's mission requires that we lay down our lives for the sake of others.

Diversity is essential for the body of Christ to function as God intended. Mentoring with a value of unity in diversity acknowledges each of us as unique creations of God, and invites us to see and experience God and each other in new ways. Dr. Martin Luther King Jr. said, "Nothing in the world is more dangerous than sincere ignorance and conscientious stupidity." Embracing diversity within a mentoring group helps us see what we can't see and know what we can't know when we worship with and have relationships only with those who share our same culture and life experiences. On the contrary, when we take the opportunity to enter into the life of someone who is unlike us, God opens our eyes to different perspectives. He causes us to reconsider our assumptions about culture, theology, and life.

When we mentor in a diverse environment, God stretches us beyond our feelings of discomfort. He challenges us to address conflict, to become peacemakers, and to live as reconciled people, not just "good people" who smile, tolerate each other, and pretend to get along. Entering mentoring relationships with those who are different from us will make us uncomfortable. While transforming us into the image of Christ, such relationships will help us surrender and see others as God sees them. Mentoring a diverse group of women forces us to keep God big and our own personal agendas small. It expands our circles of influence and opportunities for learning. It helps us not to value our own selfish ways too much, and challenges us to resist the temptation to transform others into our own image. Mentoring a diverse group of women gives us the opportunity to make a relational commitment to reflect true unity in the body of Christ.

Division in the Body

Much work remains in regard to the value of unity, reconciliation, and embracing *all* people within the body of Christ. Many churches are still divided across racial, ethnic, and socioeconomic lines. Even in our ministry programming, we segregate, isolate, and gravitate toward uniformity with those who are like us. Moms hang out with and primarily minister to other moms. College students and young professionals attend Sunday school classes together. The widows fellowship over there, while the couples and single folks sit in different ministry classrooms. Again, connecting with those of like interests and life stages is valuable, even necessary at times. But we should not make an idol of those connections or allow those connections to become a source of division in the church. We all need to humble ourselves and be intentional about connecting with people who are different from us for the sake of the gospel. A diverse mentoring experience gives us an opportunity to do just that!

From the beginning of my relationship with the Lord, his Word confirmed my expectation and his desire for us to live as reconcilers who stand together in spite of our personal differences. In the military environment, those expectations were met on a regular basis. Similarly, the gospel choir I was part of in college formed a racially and ethnically diverse community. We worshipped God together. We stood by each other and struggled together. We rejoiced when others rejoiced and mourned when our sisters and brothers mourned. We were there to encourage each other and help along the way. Some of my deepest bonds of friendship today were founded on the rock that is Christ, and centered on the devotion inherent in that environment. As Christ followers, we made a choice to love each other, embrace our differences, and grow as a spiritual family.

The church's foundation has cracks, and we must learn to value diverse relationships if the church is to grow in maturity and be a "credible witness of the gospel"[9] in today's culture. I am saddened by the lack of relational connection and mentorship among women. Conversations among writers, speakers, and ministry leaders in local congregations, seminary classrooms, and conferences across the country are filled with lamentations concerning the great divides between women in the church. Power struggles go on between older and younger generations. Ministry programming often neglects single women as well as employed and/or single mothers. I've heard many women share how they have suffered in silence, longing for a safe community in the church. They are heartbroken because no one seems to care enough to ask questions or listen to their stories and struggles. Some congregants even evaluate a mother's holiness by whether she chooses to work outside the home. Effective mentors must be observant to their ministry context so they can navigate these perceptions and divisions, and draw diverse people into nurturing mentoring relationships.

Why fight among ourselves? The truth is, we all need each other! We are our sisters' keepers! To some extent, it is important for a mentor to know that fighting among women is a direct result of the inward fighting within a universal church that generally doesn't value diversity or unity within the body of Christ. This reality presents a challenge *and* an opportunity for us. Dr. Cleveland's research reveals:

> Christians are so good at erecting division that we don't stop at the major ones (e.g., race/ethnicity, class and gender); we also create divisions *within* divisions. For example, while the body of Christ experiences significant intergender (man vs. woman) division, it is also plagued by *intra*gender (woman vs. woman and man vs. man) division.[10]

"Smaller" divisions continue in the body of Christ because we refuse to confront the major divisions within the body. By making a commitment to value unity in diversity within our mentoring relationships, however, we model a way of being for our brothers and sisters who remain divided. Whether we worship regularly at a homogenous church (where most members look like us) or a multiethnic church (which reflects the racial and ethnic differences within the body of Christ), followers of Christ must value the sacredness of our differences. Our ethnic composition is just as ordained and holy as our gender, and is at least one of the ways we reflect the image of the Triune God.

By his very nature, God being three-in-one reflects his value of unity in diversity. Christianity is a monotheistic faith; we serve one God. God the Father is God. God the Son is God. God the Holy Spirit is God. These three are one, and there is no hierarchy between them. The Son is not the Father, and he is not the Holy Spirit. The Holy Spirit is not the Father, and he is not the Son. The Father is not the Son, and he is not the Holy Spirit. The Father does not do what the Son does, the Holy Spirit has different work from the Father . . . you get the picture. This is a great mystery to us, and yet it is the holistic way we see God revealed in the Scriptures. Our diversity is indeed a reflection of the God we serve.

From the beginning of time, God created two human beings in his own image. Like the monotheistic God of all creation, he created male and female, and these two became one. Through God's own being and through the marriage of Adam and Eve, we clearly understand that *unity does not equal sameness*. True unity reflects the diversity of God who lives in harmony with himself, and he calls his image bearers to this holy living. Christ's finished work on the cross has overcome the dividing wall of hostility that causes divisions within the family of God, and his Holy Spirit is our able teacher and guide in all these family matters. We who mentor as intentional discipleship must stand with Christ, empowered by the Holy Spirit, and labor for this unity.

Christ affirms our identity so we don't have to assimilate to achieve acceptance within the body of Christ. When we affirm our identity in him, we do not reject our cultural or ethnic heritage, and we do not pretend there are no differences between genders. On the contrary, our differences within the body of Christ become a cause for celebration and a necessary contribution to the fulfillment of God's kingdom work. Once we acknowledge the contributions of our differences and commit them to the overall mission of God, only then can we truly experience the body of Christ at work and reflect God's likeness on this earth. Let there be no doubt, unity in diversity is an important principle for kingdom-minded mentoring. By humbling ourselves to see others as God sees them, we can compassionately embrace people as God does, learn from them, and welcome their contributions to the body of Christ.

Mentor for Life

1. How have your upbringing, culture, and life experiences shaped the way you view people who are from a different racial, ethnic, and/or socioeconomic background?

2. Be particularly observant as you go about your daily routine this week. Pay special attention to the traffic in your local grocery or convenience store, coffee shop, or school environment. Do you live in a diverse community? Does your local church reflect the diversity of your local community? Why or why not?

3. Revisit your potential mentoring group list from chapter 2. Is the value of unity in diversity reflected on your list? How can you intentionally invite a diverse group of women to form mentoring relationships? How might you prayerfully add to or modify this list?

4. As a mentor, how can you encourage others to embrace the value of unity in diversity and cultivate that value within your local congregation and mentoring ministry?

5. Relationship Exercise: Take the cell phone test. Review every contact in your cell phone, and make a list of your closest friends. Pay special attention to the people you interact with on a weekly and monthly basis. How many people are of a different age group, social or economic class, racial or ethnic background from you? How many have different life experiences from you? What does this exercise reveal about your value of diversity or commitment to unity?

6. Summarize in four or five sentences what you have learned from this chapter.

Tweet This

"Mentoring a diverse group of women forces us to keep God big and our own personal agendas small." #Mentor4Life @asistasjourney

Fourteen

Embrace All Women

> *Instead of casting a powerful gospel vision that both validates*
> *and mobilizes women, the church's message for women is*
> *mixed at best—guarded, negative, and small at worst.*
> **Carolyn Custis James[1]**

It is true that we become like what we see. Growing up, my gaze was constantly fixed on my mother, Sallie. She worked hard and gave everything she could so my sister and I had opportunities to thrive. She served in our church and in the community. She loved family and was always hospitable toward strangers. She was a humble woman who led—a woman of influence. Throughout her life, this woman mentored me and taught me about the importance of relationships and the humble posture of embrace—always being inviting and hospitable toward others regardless of our differences.

Because my mother was committed to serving and was free to influence others based on her passions and giftedness, nonvoters were registered, students were taught, young people remained in college, girls walked away from bad situations, families stayed together, friends found comfort, and expectations were raised. She was a woman who stood in the gap for other women.

She was liberated in her spirit and in her mind, and all who knew her were better for it. I was twenty years old when she went home to glory, but I will never forget certain things about my relationship with her. I will never forget that she found her true identity in Christ. She knew exactly who she was, and she was unwavering about embracing her calling and living her life on purpose for God.

There was a time in my adult life when well-meaning Christians wanted to close my mind to my mother's legacy, to the possibilities of what women could do to advance the kingdom of God. Some of my sisters insisted that my most important contributions would be inside my home and to my family, that everything else lacked value or relevance. Those messages stood in conflict with the testimony of my mother. As a result, I struggled to understand my identity, purpose, and calling as a woman, wife, and mother serving on active duty as an officer in the U.S. Marine Corps. I was asking myself, *What does God's Word say about women? Particularly, how does God feel about women like me?* Were my service to country and my passion to raise up future leaders less important than my family commitments? Did I have to choose between them?

Going before the Lord to wrestle with these questions and having a diverse group of mentors in Christian faith to speak into my life have helped me resolve some of these uncertainties in my own heart. Embracing my true identity in Christ meant that I had to embrace all of myself, just as God created me, and not try to fit into someone else's idea of who I should be because of my gender.

Embracing my identity in Christ also meant reflecting on the formative mentoring relationship I had with my dear mother. I am my mother's daughter, an African American woman from South Carolina who loves the Lord and his church. I am a leader, learner, teacher, servant, advocate, wife, mother, and friend. It is in this capacity that I have mentored from the perspective of intentional discipleship with a compassionate embrace of God's message for all women. Leaders in the church must ask, "Does God care about the things that concern women?" If you believe as I do that the answer to this question is yes, then let us consider what it means to effectively mentor women who understand their identity in Christ when they are diverse in their life stages, faith journeys, spiritual giftedness, professional work, and relational commitments.

Relational Connections and Finding Purpose

Understanding our identity in Christ gives us purpose. God has a specific purpose for each of us,[2] a unique calling[3] for every individual. Our shared and primary purpose is to become disciples (followers) of Jesus Christ. Our secondary callings are unique and are birthed out of our submission to the primary calling. The body of Christ misses out when we attempt to force all women into one constrained understanding of the role and responsibilities of women. Christ's transformation does not mean we blindly do as other good and godly people say we should. If we are simply content to go along just to get along, we will never come to realize our true purpose in life. A great mentor and a safe community of believers will consistently point us to Christ and challenge us to follow him as we seek clarity on our faith journeys. A godly mentor models Christ's character, while calling us to completely surrender our will and desires to God's will for our lives.

God is the creator of all things, and his creative vision is big enough to include women from all walks and stages of life, from different backgrounds and cultures. His kingdom purposes transcend generations. His will is big enough to include young girls like Rhoda, who commit themselves to prayer, and virgins like Mary, the young mother of Jesus. His plans are big enough for women like Elizabeth, Rachel, and Hannah—all of whom experienced prolonged seasons of infertility. His purposes include women with pagan pasts like Ruth, prostitutes like Rahab, and rejected, widowed, or adulterous women like the Samaritan woman at the well.[4] He sees marginalized and enslaved women like Hagar, and old women like the prophetess Anna. We compassionately embrace women like these because God's purpose and plans include all of them. God's purpose includes you as well!

Sadly, we live in a world where women constantly receive messages that communicate, *You are not valuable: You're not smart enough for this job or capable enough to earn that amount of income. You are not skinny enough to fit into those jeans. You are not attractive enough to date that guy or to have a man fully commit to only you. You're not competent enough to be a leader. You are not a great parent. You are not an excellent wife.* And when we are insecure or feel inadequate, it is easy to degrade or reject women who are either more confident than we are or who have made different choices from our own. This rejection somehow makes us feel better about ourselves and more comfortable with our choices, if only for a moment.

Does this happen in the church? Of course it does. This monster rears its ugly head in the guise of comparison and envy. In a shallow attempt to feel better about ourselves, women play games of one-upmanship. This *intra*gender division referenced in Dr. Cleveland's research reveals that we lack confidence in our own skills, abilities, and choices, and our identity in Christ is not secure. As a result, we add to the mounting list of things our sisters in Christ "should" be doing to gain *our* approval and acceptance. Young, single girls should go to college or to the mission field. Married women should have children (and the more they have, the better). Mothers tend to get an extra wink for staying at home or choosing to homeschool. And what about the multitudes of women—some lost, some barren, some college students, some single, some old, some divorced, some widows, some single mothers—who come to church and sit on the sidelines waiting for someone to notice them and invite them in? These women are no different from me in that they want embracing and they need encouragement and direction concerning their role in God's kingdom.

The more I learn, the better I understand that God reveals his will for each of our lives in very specific ways at opportune times. In my own life, I find he often clarifies direction within the context of Christian community. In other words, my spiritual gift of leadership was not given to me so I can have a long title behind my name or earn a great paycheck. Don't get me wrong; those can be nice benefits. The gifts of God, however, are given for serving the people of God, and it is for this reason and purpose that I labor. There is a significant difference between living my life on purpose and aimlessly moving through life without direction. I am able to do the former because I have been embraced and nurtured within Christian communities where God was clearly at work. First, I committed to the primary calling of being a disciple and follower of Christ, and only then did I get clarity about my purpose or role in God's kingdom.

The Word Made Plain

The biblical narrative makes it clear that God does not call all women to the same choices or life paths; however, he does call us all to follow him. He does call us all to a united Christian community. Our spiritual journeys are really about serving a God who is good, and about knowing without a shadow of doubt that through Christ's finished work on the cross, we are made righteous before that same God. Through salvation, God himself has done a great work in us. Our faith tells us he has great plans for us. Because of our faith and through the power of the Holy Spirit, we are equipped to persevere and to work. In spite of our challenges and our suffering, we can live with power, hope, and joy as he intends. Mentoring can be a catalyst God uses to deepen our relational commitment to other women and to his church. Mentoring as intentional discipleship affirms our true identity in Christ and reminds us of the power of the Holy Spirit at work in community through us.

To practice this theological truth, we must understand God's loving message and posture of embrace toward *all* women:

- *To the single women: Your singleness is a gift from the Lord, even when it doesn't feel that way. Be generous with your gifts, and treasure the time God has given for you to worship him without distraction.*

- *To the wives: God doesn't just want to change your husband to give him a hope and future. God wants to transform you as well. Look up in reverence to God. Watch and pray.*

- *To the widows: God understands you have suffered an extreme loss. Take time to grieve and care for your soul, and understand that your loss is not the end of your journey. God still has a purpose for you, and he will comfort you and give you peace.*

- *To the single mothers: God sees you! Like Hagar lost in the desert with a crying baby and no resources, God will provide for you and your children. Trust him and obey.*

- *To the barren women: God is with you in your trial. He accepts you, and you will be fruitful for his kingdom. Throughout the Bible, God used countless faithful women—like Miriam; the prophetess Huldah; Mary of Bethany; Priscilla—and we don't know if they ever had children.*

- *To the mothers: You are not in charge of your children's salvation. God is. After a certain point in life, you are not even responsible for their choices. They are. Model for them a life devoted to God, train them, and release them to God's care.*

- *To the women who work outside the home: Like Deborah and the model of the Proverbs 31 woman, God has enlarged your territory. Do not take your opportunities to influence lightly. Glorify God in your work.*

- *To the older women: There is no such thing as "retiring" from God's kingdom work. Run your race faithfully until the end. Walk, roll, or limp if necessary, but don't give up on this journey!*

Remain faithful and diligent. Take women under your wings and be an example of how to finish well!

- *To the younger women: Respect your elders. Sit at their feet and learn from them. There is nothing new under the sun (Eccl. 1:9).*
- *To all God's daughters everywhere: We have a responsibility to remember our identity in Christ and the work of the Lord in our lives.*

Since we are all created in the image of God, we must compassionately embrace God's message for all women.

Mentoring across Generations

As we embrace God's message for all women, we also value the relationships cultivated across generations. We serve a God who cares about generations. Throughout the first five books of the Bible, he constantly refers to himself as the "God of Abraham, Isaac, and Jacob."[5] He has a historical plan and fulfills that plan across generations. To agree with God as people of faith means we must invest in mentoring, discipling, and cultivating Christian character and leadership across generations. The word *remember* echoed in Moses' instructions throughout the Israelite camp because God expected the elderly, the wise, and the spiritually mature to teach their children and their children's children about Yahweh (God)—both who he was and what he had done. The purpose of this training or remembering was also so the elderly did not forget. At least part of the reason the Israelites persisted in sin is because the people did not remember and the elderly did not teach!

Writers of the Psalms clearly share the blessings that follow those who teach across generations. "Let this be written for a future generation, that a people not yet created may praise the LORD" (Ps. 102:18). Also, "From everlasting to everlasting the LORD's love is with those who fear him, and his righteousness with their children's children—with those who keep his covenant and remember to obey his precepts" (Ps. 103:17–18). Therefore, making relational commitments to teach and share the Word of God across generations is paramount.

The year I started studying and thinking about mentoring from the perspective of intentional discipleship, I paid particular attention to the cross-generational relationship between Naomi and Ruth. Although Naomi was older and a daughter of Abraham, sometimes she was weak, had lost hope and focus, and needed Ruth. Ruth's willingness to abandon her family and pagan heritage to follow Naomi speaks volumes about the will and purpose of God to transform lives even in difficult circumstances. It was Ruth who provided for Naomi's physical needs. Once Naomi's faith was restored, she and Ruth partnered together in a courageous act of love and devotion to have Naomi's husband's name restored, which was a proper act of service. Their relationship was mutually beneficial: one was old and one was young; one knew Yahweh and the other initially did not know him; one was physically and emotionally strong when the other was weak. Regardless of our ages, mentoring across generational lines can be a blessing to all involved.

This Is How We Do It

We embrace all women and mentor across generations so that women of all ages will learn from each other. Mentoring across generations means we intentionally place older and younger women in the same mentoring groups, but we also intentionally diversify our mentoring groups in other ways. After the women complete a brief information form[6] at the beginning of the mentoring season, we prayerfully place older and younger, married and single, employed and stay-at-home moms in the same mentoring groups. For all the reasons mentioned in these two chapters, we are intentional about pursuing the value of unity in diversity within mentoring groups. In a diverse mentoring group, everyone is valued and everyone contributes. Mentoring in this way benefits every woman involved. After almost five years of watching women grow in the mentoring ministry, I am still amazed by how much women are stretched and how much they learn in a diverse mentoring environment.

One of the mentees in the women's mentoring ministry provided this testimony:

> I came away with many blessings, one of which was being a part of a diverse group of believers. I found it helpful to listen to the views of ladies in other seasons of life than my own. I would sometimes benefit from the wisdom of a more mature believer, and sometimes it was the fresh eyes of a new disciple that I needed to look to for perspective and understanding.

In addition to intentionally diversifying mentoring groups, we want to make the opportunity to commit as easy as possible. Out of respect for people's schedules, we offer mentoring group opportunities at different times and in various home locations throughout the month. It is not considerate to ask busy women to come to a mentoring group across town on a weeknight, so we carefully consider the mentee's geographical location and times of availability when placing her in a mentoring group. We provide the address and gathering times on our information form, and we ask the mentees to select their top three options based on their own schedules and location. We intentionally do *not* provide the mentors' names because we don't want mentees making group selections based on the mentors they personally like. We also do not tell them what mentoring resources we will use for mentoring groups because we do not want them to reject the opportunity if they have preconceived notions about a particular book or its author. This process also ensures mentees are not selecting groups based on their friendship circles or life stages. From the very beginning, we try to stretch women outside of their comfort zones.

One mentee confessed:

> God has taken a group of ladies from various backgrounds and of various ages and created an environment where together we can grow closer to him while encouraging each other. What an honor it has been to pray for my sisters in Christ and to see God actively working in their lives.

Out of the diversity of our groups, God brings great unity. We encourage this by:

- Intentionally providing a safe mentoring community for all women.
- Affirming that God has purposely made each of us differently; therefore, we affirm that *unity in diversity* glorifies God.
- Teaching that God has a gospel message that includes all his daughters.
- Looking beyond ourselves to *see* and compassionately embrace others.
- Making Jesus the top priority and focus of our mentoring relationships.
- Praying, praying, and praying some more.

We make the relational commitment to embrace people as God does and welcome diverse relationships that reflect true unity in the body of Christ. We do this because unity in diversity is important to God. After all, that is his very nature. He is one God of three diverse persons, the perfect blend of unity in diversity. This is what relational harmony looks like in the body of Christ.

Mentor for Life

1. In what ways are you connected to women across various generations? Can you think of a woman from each generation with whom you connect regularly? List their names, noting what drew you to them and what sustains your relationship.

2. What conclusions have you drawn about the responsibilities and choices of women? How has this chapter challenged your views?

3. How can you prepare to effectively mentor women who have made life choices different from yours? How is it helpful to embrace the understanding that mentoring will be a mutually beneficial relationship?

4. Remember: Can you articulate specific ways your life experiences and relationships have shaped you? How do these experiences equip you to mentor a diverse group of women?

5. Relationship Exercise: Watch a documentary that directly confronts injustices against women in the world. Journal about what you learned from the exercise. Identify the beliefs that undergird the injustice. How does God's Word speak life and hope into these situations? How does this experience better shape your understanding of what women are up against, and how does this exposure help you embrace all of God's women?

6. Summarize in four or five sentences what you have learned from this chapter.

Tweet This

"Mentoring can be the catalyst God uses to deepen our relational commitment to other women and to his church." #Mentor4Life @asistasjourney

Mentoring

A Commitment to Love

Let us be women who carry each other.
Let us be women who give from what we have.
Let us be women who leap to do the difficult things,
the unexpected things and the necessary things.
Let us be women who live for Peace.
Let us be women who breathe Hope.
Let us be women who create beauty.
Let us be women who Love . . .
Let us rise to the questions of our time.
Let us speak to the injustices in our world.
Let us move the mountains of fear and intimidation.
Let us shout down the walls that separate and divide.
Let us fill the earth with the fragrance of Love.
Let us be women who Love.

Idelette McVicker[1]

Christ's love is sacrificial, obedient, and centered on God's will.

Mentoring as intentional discipleship is a continuous, sacrificial, and selfless act that shapes our character, clarifies our spiritual gifts, and affirms our purpose and calling.

Fifteen

Obedience and Sacrifice

Greater love has no one than this: to lay down one's life for one's friends.

Jesus[1]

I've been convicted. I don't always value the gift of play. When I am about to go on a phone conference or head to a meeting, or if I am struggling to get dinner on the table or to clean house, or even if I am in the middle of sending an email or completing a task, that is inevitably the very moment my daughter wants me to stop and play. I don't always stop. Sometimes I feel like I sacrifice the time and interruption out of obligation because I am Mom.

The truth is, I can think of a long list of things I would rather do than shape Play-Doh. But when I sacrifice my will to surrender to her felt needs, she feels loved. I am reminded in that shared time and space with her that I am loved as well. Through my daughter, God reminds me of his gifts of play, rest, slowing down, and spontaneity. This is the way *she* mentors *me*. And I can't receive these gifts if I don't sacrifice my will and soften some of the discipline I have learned through military training.

Completing military training was very difficult. As a woman and as a Christian, I struggled with feelings of inadequacy and displacement. Compared to the guys, I wasn't strong enough or fast enough. I hated living half the time in "the field," where we ate, slept, and disposed of our bodily fluids outside. It was evident early on that my biggest contribution to the Marine Corps was not going to be my physical stamina or my ability to overpower another human being. Being an officer was really a call to service—service to God, the Marine Corps, and my country. It was a call to defend the values of our nation and her people and to preserve the lives of those I considered friends.

In officer's training, I found it difficult to embrace my fellow Marines as intimate friends. In some cases, I secretly wondered if they were chemically imbalanced. The longer we stayed in the field, the more I learned about them. Some of them reveled in the harsh and rigorous training. I, on the other hand, preferred living inside, eating hot meals, using clean restrooms, and taking warm showers. Those miserable training days were filled with my grumblings and complaints. I just wanted it all to be over! Then, on a hot summer day during a military exercise in 2002 (a little more than a year after the September 11, 2001, terrorist attack), it finally dawned on me: *We are indeed a country at war. Who cares how imbalanced some of my peers may seem? At the end of the day, I want to fight next to the person who is willing to sacrifice his or her life to get me home.* This mental and emotional shift helped me better trust the men and women with whom I had the privilege of serving. My new understanding allowed me to visualize us as interdependent people with a united mission. Through this change in thinking, I began to see my peers as friends.

True friends are not just people you enjoy being around. They are people you have committed to love—people you will sacrificially give yourself to care for and to protect. True friends are people you can depend on. Jesus speaks of this when he uses the metaphor of bearing fruit as an image of discipleship. He said:

As the Father has loved me, so have I loved you. Now remain in my love. If you keep my commands, you will remain in my love, just as I have kept my Father's commands and remain in his love. . . . My command is this: Love each other as I have loved you. Greater love has no one than this: to lay down one's life for one's friends. You are my friends if you do what I command. I no longer call you servants, because a servant does not know his master's business. Instead, I have called you friends, for everything that I learned from my Father I have made known to you. You did not choose me, but I chose you and appointed you so that you might go and bear fruit—fruit that will last. (John 15:9–10, 12–16)

These passages reveal a great deal about mentoring as intentional discipleship, and what it means to live on mission for God. We first learn that Jesus served and taught because he was motivated by love. Because he freely received love from his Father, Jesus freely shared his love with others. Jesus' commitment to do his Father's will communicated the sanctity of his love. We also learn that our love for God and our obedience to him are intimately connected. When we don't obey God's instructions for living, our disobedience is a direct indicator that our love is defective. Likewise, by keeping his commands, we continue to dwell in his love.[2] Finally, we see that true love is demonstrated by a willingness to give of ourselves, to sacrifice for the sake of others.

Jesus' Motivation on Display

The scene in John 15 was not the first time Jesus shared these principles or lived sacrificially among his disciples. John 4 reveals that he was tired and thirsty by the time he went through Samaria, where he sat and chatted with a Samaritan woman. He was also hungry, which is why his disciples went into town to buy food. But when they returned with sustenance, the nourishment they thought he needed, he replied, "I have food to eat that you know nothing about" (John 4:32). Upon hearing this, the disciples were undoubtedly as confused as we are after first reading the verse. But then he settled their anxiety, at least for a moment: "'My food,' said Jesus, 'is to do the will of him who sent me and to finish his work'" (v. 34). This language sounds just like a U.S. Marine responding to the military orders of his commanding officer. Although Jesus was tired, hungry, and thirsty, he pressed on to continue his work. He did everything possible to complete his mission, and he laid down his life to get the job done.

After he healed a blind man, Jesus again reminded his disciples, "As long as it is day, we must do the work of him who sent me" (John 9:4). The apostle John records the heart of Jesus' motivation as his earthly ministry and life drew near its end. Jesus prayed to his Father, "I have brought you glory on earth by finishing the work you gave me to do" (John 17:4). Jesus' death and sacrifice on the cross was simply his final act of obedience.

Some people minister and urge others to follow Christ by focusing on the negative, saying things like, "Will you go to Heaven or Hell when you die? If you commit [this sin], you can be assured of negative consequences and the wrath of God." No doubt there is great wisdom in fleeing from sin. Yet Christ gives us another method to encourage people toward right living and right action. He casts a positive vision by encouraging his disciples to open their eyes and see:

> Look at the fields! They are ripe for harvest. . . . the saying "One sows and another reaps" is true. I sent you to reap what you have not worked for. Others have done the hard work, and you have reaped the benefits of their labor. (John 4:35, 37–38)

Here, Jesus is using his listeners' understanding of planting and growing (they lived in a primarily agricultural economy) to impart a spiritual truth: the kingdom of God has come, and souls are now being gathered into it! The harvest is abundant! It is the sign of a new age, a fulfillment of the promises made during the time of the patriarchs, judges, prophets, and kings. Jesus is essentially saying that the foundation for the kingdom has been set, and the hard work has already been done. They are the beneficiaries of the work, and all they have to do is gather the harvest. This is a message of hope—a vision to help them see what is possible, the positive consequences of their obedience and commitment to the Father's will. We know and understand the unintended negative consequences of sin, and yet we must also acknowledge the blessings that come with obedience and a sacrificial commitment to Christ. The work of gathering a plentiful harvest is to bring us great joy!

The Samaritan woman had an encounter with Jesus. She left the well unashamed and unselfish, and she sacrificially gave her testimony in a small act of obedience. From her testimony, many people in the town were saved. This opened the gateway for Jesus to teach, and a revival broke out! In the same way, there are always beneficiaries to our faithful obedience and commitment to God; oftentimes they are more abundant than we will ever know or understand this side of heaven. Some plant, some water, and some get the increase. Make the sacrifice to the glory of God.

Love in Action

In the same way Jesus was motivated by his love for the Father, love is our motivation for obeying God. Jesus does not mince words when he states, "If you love me, keep me commands" (John 14:15). The apostle John records this statement five times in various forms, three times from the lips of Jesus.[3] He writes in 1 John 5:2–4:

This is how we know that we love the children of God: by loving God and carrying out his commands. In fact, this is love for God: to keep his commands. And his commands are not burdensome, for everyone born of God overcomes the world. This is the victory that has overcome the world, even our faith.

John writes clearly of how our commitment to the Great Commandment is on display. We know we truly love the people of God when we love God and keep his commandments. The two are inseparable. Likewise, our love for God and our obedience to him are inseparable. After making these connections, John follows the model of his Savior by giving a positive analogy and a hopeful vision: "This is the victory that has overcome the world, even our faith. Who is it that overcomes the world? Only the one who believes that Jesus is the Son of God" (1 John 5:4–5). This is good news! Those who are committed to mentoring must not shy away from the truth that God has called all his true disciples to sacrificially give up their old lives and old manners of being in exchange for new lives in Christ.

Love and Obedience

We must learn obedience, and it's not always easy. Hebrews 5:7–9 reads:

> During the days of Jesus' life on earth, he offered up prayers and petitions with fervent cries and tears to the one who could save him from death, and he was heard because of his reverent submission. Son though he was, he learned obedience from what he suffered and, once made perfect, he became the source of eternal salvation for all who obey him.

The author of Hebrews tells us that even Christ learned obedience through his suffering. God does not waste anything in our lives. He uses all things, even our sacrifice and our suffering, to draw us closer to him. In his suffering, Jesus offered prayers and petitions, cries and tears to the One who shared his life. He learned obedience through his willingness to lay down his life and serve the Father. The same is true for us. Our love for God calls us to obedience, sacrifice, and submission.

Several months after the mentoring ministry first began, one of the mentors confessed she was having difficulty connecting with the other ladies in her group. Misperceptions and insecurities robbed this woman of her confidence in Christ's ability to use her as a leader. Unfortunately, one of the older women in the group would not accept the mentor's counsel, and even though they both consistently showed up for the monthly group gathering, the relationship between the two was strained. Neither one of them confronted the issue, so months passed without resolution. The relationship remained difficult and cold.

This mentor desired to see God work in a mighty way, so she submitted the issue to God and surrendered her desires in prayer. She prayed that God would allow her mentee to listen, to learn, and to receive her love. She prayed, hoping to find a way to break the distrust, and was convicted that God was calling her to demonstrate the sacrificial love of Christ. During prayer, God led her to meditate and reflect on John 13:1–17, where Jesus demonstrated his love and servant leadership by washing the disciples' feet. She shares:

> After meditating on the passage, I began to fret that Jesus was asking me to wash my mentees' feet, not because he was teaching this practice as a command for all of his disciples, but rather because through this demonstration, Jesus showed his humility, his love, and his servant's heart. For the record, I don't like feet! I don't care for my own feet, and I certainly don't want to touch the feet of others! It seemed unthinkable that God would give me the desire to wash the feet of eight women!

But I continued to read and reread the passage, and saw the impact that this foot washing had on the disciples. God quietly nudged me with verse 15, "I have set you an example that you should do as I have done for you." This call to obedience meant that I had to wash their feet. God wanted me to physically demonstrate that I wasn't mentoring because I had more experience. I was mentoring to serve these, his women and my sisters.

Despite her fears, this woman decided to wash the feet of the other women in her mentoring group, including the older woman with whom she had experienced conflict. In this sacrificial act of obedience, she modeled a love of Christ that is centered on God's will. She continues:

God was humbling me, as I washed those beautiful feet and prayed for each of the mentees. Because we had already spent so much time together, my prayers were specific and purposeful. I tenderly grasped the feet of the woman I had difficulty reaching and offered prayers to God as the purifying water dripped through the cracks in her feet. Tears began to roll down her cheeks. Then, softly and subtly, I heard the words of her prayers as she asked God to forgive her for having such a hard heart toward me, for not allowing me to minster to her, and for her unwillingness to see past my age. God so mercifully and graciously allowed this foot washing to literally wash away the wall that divided us for so many months.

This act of obedience serves as a reflection of what it means to live as a fruit-bearing servant of Christ. Our connection to Christ teaches us to sacrificially and selflessly love others. Mentoring is a continuous selfless act that teaches us how to love, shapes our character, and affirms our purpose.

The Commission

In John 15, Jesus is preparing his disciples to launch. He no longer calls them servants because servants do not know their master's business. He calls them friends because he has taught them everything he learned from the Father. Likewise, the people God calls us to mentor are not our servants. Their purpose in being present is not to meet our needs or to satisfy our desires. Mentees are peers and friends we are called to serve. By serving them, we reject our personal agendas and bring the master's business or kingdom mission into focus. Through teaching and training, mentors and mentees better understand God, his good purposes for all creation, and the privilege we have to join in his redemptive work. We sacrifice together in order for the master's work to go forth.

Jesus reveals that he chose his disciples to go and bear fruit that will last. The metaphor of bearing fruit is regularly used in the New Testament to communicate a changed life. Only a good tree (a person who is rooted and grounded in Christ) can bear good fruit[4] that will last.[5] Mentors and mentees alike must encourage each other to persevere and continually bear lasting fruit.

Discipleship is a command of God. As obedient servants and friends of God, we make disciples whose lives are fruitful and productive for fulfilling God's kingdom mission because only what we do for God has eternal value. Mentoring is a call to action, a call to fight, and our greatest weapon of warfare is our commitment to love.[6] This is Jesus' commandment: "Lay down your life" (John 15:13) and "Love each other as I have loved you" (John 15:12).

A commitment to love others is at the core of everything we do:

> God is love. This is how God showed his love among us: He sent his one and only Son into the world that we might live through him. This is love: not that we loved God, but that he loved us and sent his Son as an atoning sacrifice for our sins.

Dear friends, since God so loved us, we also ought to love one another. (1 John 4:8–11)

God showed his love for us by sending his Son into the world. We affirm this sacrificial love by loving God and loving others. Make the sacrifice.

After he sacrificially ministered, taught, practiced, and walked among them, Jesus commissioned his disciples and sent them into the world. What does it look like to send people out as disciples into the world? It means we practice what we have been taught with our words and with right actions. Dr. Maya Angelou had a wise saying: "When you learn, teach."[7] Good mentors understand that students or mentees must be prepared to eventually become leaders or teachers of others.[8] Mentors must consistently challenge their mentees, persuade them to take risks, to practice, to live lives of integrity, to sacrifice, and to start over when they fail. Mentors inspire mentees to *be fully themselves* for the sake of the kingdom.

Those being mentored will eventually assume the role of teacher. And if they have been trained well, they will become wise, humble, and thoughtful mentors and servant leaders themselves. *To mentor for life* is the commitment. Life transformation that honors God is the goal. You, too, can find your purpose through intentional discipleship.

Mentor for Life

1. In what areas of life might God be calling you to discipline yourself or sacrificially lay down your life for the sake of another person?

2. What do we learn from Jesus' teaching and character from the featured texts in the gospel of John?

3. How does Jesus' teaching in the featured verses of John 15 help prepare your heart to mentor?

4. How will you be intentional about speaking the truth in love and sharing a positive vision for mentees to under-stand God's best for his children?

5. Love Exercise: Are there areas in your life where your actions do not reflect a true love of God? Name them. Turn this list into a prayer. Find a safe person to share this with, and ask them to assist you in surrendering these areas to God.

6. Summarize in four or five sentences what you have learned from this chapter.

Tweet This

"Our love not only calls us to obedience, it also calls us to submission." #Mentor4Life @asistasjourney

Sixteen

Spiritual Gifts and Christian Character

When we practice surrendered, obedient faith, we will
experience the movement of the Spirit.
Robertson McQuilkin[1]

God gives each of us spiritual gifts. He assigns us purposeful work that accomplishes what he wants. We see this in the life of the apostle Paul, when God calls him to ministry in Acts 9:15. God says to Ananias, "Go! This man [we know as Paul] is my chosen instrument to proclaim my name to the Gentiles and their kings and to the people of Israel." Just like that, Paul is commissioned to join God's mission. Like Paul, God has created each of us for a specific purpose, and he has given us each different passions, talents, abilities, and skills to complete the good works he has prepared (Eph. 2:10).

While we possess certain skills and talents naturally, we all have spiritual gifts as well. These are diverse, but they all have an ultimate purpose. That purpose is to join with other believers to collectively labor and love so God's will can be done on earth. First Corinthians 12 is the most exhaustive passage on the topic of spiritual gifts. Paul begins the discussion by sharing the importance of unity in the body of Christ:

> There are different kinds of gifts, but the same Spirit distributes them. There are different kinds of service, but the same Lord. There are different kinds of working, but in all of them and in everyone it is the same God at work. Now to each one the manifestation of the Spirit is given for the common good. (1 Cor. 12:4–7)

When we are surrendered, humble, and obedient, the power of the Holy Spirit works through us to fulfill God's purposes in the world. In this passage, we learn that not all of us have the same spiritual gifts. God has gifted us differently on purpose, and therefore, we are not to covet one another's spiritual gifts. On the contrary, we encourage the active use of each other's gifts for their contributions to the body of Christ, and we cultivate our own spiritual gifts to that end.

What are spiritual gifts, and why are they important for mentoring as intentional discipleship? Spiritual gifts are talents, skills, and functions of God's grace to us, as an extension of our faith in him (Eph. 2:8–9; 4:7–8). These spiritual gifts are generally recognized and affirmed in a community where people know us well. The community benefits from the use of our gifts. Spiritual gifts serve the specific purpose of preparing God's people "for works of service, so that the body of Christ may be built up until we all reach unity in the faith and in the knowledge of the Son of God and become mature, attaining to the whole measure of the fullness of Christ" (Eph. 4:12–13). It is easy for an undisciplined person who lacks maturity to use his or her giftedness to seek praise, isolation, or elevation above others because of pride. This is a temptation for all of us who are good in a particular area. This passage, however, reminds us of the importance of the priority and focus of our spiritual gifts.

Our spiritual gifts are for the edification of the body. This is an important understanding for anyone who wants to mentor as intentional discipleship, because any gifts or talents you use in the

218 The Mentoring Commitment

areas of your life not considered "ministry," you can also use to benefit the body of Christ. This opens the doors of opportunity for how you lead and serve in your local congregation, and most important, how you invite your mentees and congregants to collectively lead and serve your local community. Mentors know their spiritual gifts, and they observe, affirm, and nurture the spiritual gifts of others. This awareness and understanding brings unity and strength to the body of Christ.

I remember growing up in small churches where the saints of God would praise and affirm the truths of God. In the South, we would sing lyrics like, "Whatever you need, God got it!" As an adult, I grew in confidence of that simple affirmation. Whatever the people of God need to do the work of God, God knows all about it; he will often meet those needs through other people, with the skills, talents, gifts, and resources that are already in the body. Frequently, we do not have because we have not observed, we have not affirmed, we have not trained, and we have not asked.[2]

This, too, is the continuous action and work of mentoring. When we utilize our spiritual gifts for the edification of the body of Christ, we are actually honoring and worshipping God. We are also acknowledging our need for community, because none of our spiritual gifts is fully functional in isolation. Preachers need administrators, and administrators need helpers. Those who speak in tongues need interpreters. Those with the gifts of wisdom and knowledge need the support and community of able teachers. Prophets need the creativity of artists, and poets need the words of prophets to create beauty to the glory of God. All of us operating in our giftedness together clarifies our purpose and affirms our calling.

Mentoring can help people discern their spiritual gifts, passions, and talents, and through the leadership of the Holy Spirit, somehow bring those gifts together for the common good. Paul says that we should not be uninformed concerning spiritual gifts (2 Cor 12:1), because we all have different kinds of gifts, services, and work for the kingdom. It is true, some of us will inevitably be better at certain tasks than others, and that's exactly how God designed his church to function (1 Cor. 12:18)—so that each part will mutually edify and complement the others (1 Cor. 12:21–26). Therefore, we must not be reluctant to utilize the spiritual gift(s) God has given us, and we need not devalue or covet the spiritual gifts of others.

The important teaching to remember is this: there is one Spirit, one Lord, and one God who works in and through his children. He gives us gifts of his spirit for the common good of human-kind, and not for us to boast about how great we are. Through the diversity and connectedness of our spiritual gifts, we find ways to collectively and effectively bear witness to the gospel. Paul continues this teaching by encouraging the believers in Corinth to eagerly desire the greater gifts of faith, hope, and love—with love being the supreme manifestation of the work of the Holy Spirit and the revelation of God.

To escape the responsibility of mentoring, some women say, "I am not gifted in that area," or "I don't feel called." But making disciples is *not* a spiritual gift. It is not something unique that only certain people are called to do. *All* Christians are called to this important kingdom work! Teaching and training are crucial for equipping others to cultivate their abilities to mentor. Given the power and work of the Holy Spirit, should we choose to accept them, many of us can grow in our areas of weakness and become competent and effective mentors.

Spiritual Gifts Build Up the Body of Believers

Spiritual gifts are the means through which works of righteousness are completed in the church and beyond. Paul's writing about the purpose of spiritual gifts in Ephesians 4:8–13 gives us a focus on which to meditate. This passage reveals the hope and prayer we have when we mentor and disciple people for God's kingdom purposes. Thankfully, we are not alone in this work. Paul informs us that God himself does the transformative work in us so we do not remain spiritual babies, but rather grow up or mature in Christ Jesus (Eph. 4:14–15). From Christ, "the whole body, joined and held together by every supporting ligament, grows and builds itself up in love, as *each part* does its work" (Eph. 4:16, emphasis mine). Our spiritual gifts advance *our understanding of God*, his grace and his power—the first pillar of the mentoring framework. Through our individual service and obedience, the church is collectively strengthened and united and we all, together, become what God intended. This is the Holy Spirit's work of *sanctification*[3] *in us*, as mentoring affirms the identity of the whole person in Christ—the second pillar of the mentoring framework. Finally, we experience the Holy Spirit's work of *sanctification through us*, as mentoring equips us to love others well—the third pillar of the mentoring framework.

The Gift of Grace and the Development of Christian Character

In Titus chapter 2, the apostle Paul writes to his mentee, Titus, to inform him of what is true for *all* Christians. The context of the passage speaks to the importance of developing our Christian character by reminding us of God's grace at work in our hearts.

The grace of God "teaches us to say 'No' to ungodliness and worldly passions, and to live self-controlled, upright and godly lives in this present age . . . [for God desires] to purify for himself a people that are his very own, eager to do what is good" (Titus 2:12–14). In everything, we are to set an example by doing what is right. We must teach by showing integrity, seriousness, and soundness of judgment. These are the character-shaping elements

Paul champions, and they are just as true for disciples who seek to follow Jesus today.

Paul understood that the gospel is not simply about what we have been saved *from*, but also about what we have been called *to*. We have been saved for a purpose; we have been called to live a life that is self-controlled, upright, and godly in this present age. The gift of salvation makes us people of character so we can set an example for others and do what is right. The gift of salvation makes us people of integrity who judge rightly. The gift of salvation compels us to love. Christ's love is sacrificial, obedient, and centered on God's will. Our commitment to mentoring as intentional discipleship affirms our love for God and our love for other people.

What shapes the character of a mentor? The work of God in her heart and the choices she makes. Mentors commit to knowing and loving God intimately. They commit to affirming their identity in Christ. This includes being honest with themselves and others, and passionately living out their calling as daughters of the Creator of the universe. This includes fleeing from sin and walking in freedom. This means fearlessly rejecting the lies of the Enemy and standing on the Word of truth. This means graciously loving themselves just as God created them. Mentoring means being generous—sharing the same grace and love that we have received with others. It means giving all of ourselves—our minds, souls, gifts, passions, and talents—as an offering back to God to use as he sees fit. It is a sacrifice, a call to lay down our lives for God's kingdom mission and for the sake of others. It is a call to surrender every day, making the choice to pursue greatness instead of what seems easy, comfortable, and good. This type of love is a life-altering decision. This type of love is sacrificial. This type of love is an obedient commitment. This type of love shapes our character.

This Is How We Do It

When we think about the mentoring commitment to love, we are considering our willingness to sacrifice and obey God, whether we will use our spiritual gifts to benefit the body of Christ, and whether we will grow in Christian character. When we consider our commitment to love, we are really contemplating whether we will live as people of integrity. This book articulates the accountability and support a mentoring group can provide to help us live fully surrendered to God. I pray that the personal examples and chapter exercises will assist you in cultivating this desire.

Using Our Spiritual Gifts

We encourage mentees in practical ways to recognize and use their spiritual gifts to bless the body of Christ. One of the first exercises we ask mentees to complete is a spiritual gift inventory. This is a tool very similar to a personality test. In my experience, many mentees have never taken one before and have no understanding of what their unique contribution to God's kingdom could be. A spiritual gifts inventory can provide some sense of direction and an approximation of a person's spiritual gifts, but it is not the ultimate authority. The results must make sense. For example, it is unlikely that you will have the spiritual gift of teaching if you dread the thought of speaking in front of people. The person with the spiritual gift of teaching will get excited about the opportunity of imparting wisdom and knowledge into the lives of others. Likewise, if the inventory results say that you have the spiritual gift of hospitality, but you don't like being around people, don't put too much weight on those results. Consider the other gifts that are highlighted as well. An inventory is a tool, but it is not always entirely accurate.

When people are trying to determine their spiritual gifts, I normally ask two questions: (1) what are you passionate about, and (2) what are you good at? The place where the answers to those two questions intersect will most likely reflect their true spiritual gift(s). If you don't have a passion for or are not good at something, it is probably a good indicator you are not gifted in that area. Again, your spiritual gifts will most likely be affirmed in Christian community.

Having a spiritual gift does not mean, however, that you don't still need to grow and develop in that area. In fact, the opposite is true. Even though you are gifted in an area, you must seek additional training to grow and develop the gifts God has given to you. This commitment is a matter of stewarding your God-given gifts well. Along the same lines, just because you are not spiritually gifted in an area does not mean you cannot cultivate that gift or talent to serve in the kingdom of God. At various times in life, many of us will be forced into situations and circumstances simply because there is an emergency or resources are limited. Sometimes we serve because we are present and there is an identified need, regardless of our spiritual gifts, desires, or abilities. Being a parent is a great example of this. Very few people feel fully prepared to be a mother or father, but once a baby arrives, you are present in that situation and you get on-the-job training. You are suddenly a mother—now you must grow and learn. So don't use your gifts or lack thereof as an excuse to avoid serving the body of Christ.

The commitment to love encourages us to grow in Christian character. There is no silver bullet or magic formula that will produce this result. The Holy Spirit does this work. Remember the Samaritan woman Jesus sat with at the well? Once she had an encounter with Jesus, her whole life changed. She knew it in the core of her being and ran off to tell everybody in town about it. Her change was immediate, and yet I'm sure she still had much to learn. Her miraculous encounter with Jesus and her testimony were only the beginning of her growth in Christian character. She, like us, had to continue on her faith journey. The old folks in my hometown would say, "Just keep on livin' baby."

Sharing Our Testimonies

There is power in our testimonies! The fact that God would change anyone's heart is nothing short of a miracle. We acknowledge the authority of the Holy Spirit that transforms lives when we rejoice in God-honoring testimonies. As a matter of hope and a blessed assurance of the promises we have received from God, testimonies form our lives and shape our character.

In our normal, healthy, comfortable lives, we can easily grow blind to our need for God's presence and mercy. We can be deceived into boastful thinking that our good deeds or religious activity is what makes us acceptable to God—like we are doing God a favor and that's what gets his approval. It is humbling to recognize that there is absolutely nothing we can do to reach God. The blessing and benefit of the gospel is that the Creator of the universe decided to come down and be present with us. And it is his good pleasure to invite us to join in his great work. So we don't testify for others to see how good we are, what we have done, how dark our past is, or where we have come from. We testify to boast of the goodness and grace of the Lord, and to give honor and praise where it is due. We testify to remind ourselves and others how desperately we need God. Obediently and selflessly sharing our testimonies is a sacrificial deed, and it is through the power of testimony that we are encouraged and changed.

Where Do We Go from Here?

Once we, as mentors, have fulfilled the mentoring commitments of presence, discipline, mission, community, relationships, and love, there is only one thing left to do. We need to know when to let go. At some point, we will all come to a crossroad in our mentoring relationships. When we reach that crossroad, some may be compelled to ask, "What happens after our mentoring relationship comes to an end?" When God makes it clear the season of mentoring has ended, mentors and mentees can reflect on their time together and thank him. After a time of reflection, mentors can encourage those they mentor to move forward into their next phase of life and ministry. Mentors must affirm and bless their mentees. This transition will undoubtedly include a challenge and a charge for mentees to become mentors themselves. Mentors multiply. Since mentoring is not about us, we are called to teach and train mentees, and to be sensitive to God's nudge when it is time to release mentees and let them go. Seeing this growth and change is perhaps the greatest joy for any mentor.

Because our God has demonstrated his love toward us through sacrifice and obedience, we can sacrificially lay down our lives for the sake of others and for the sake of his kingdom. As mentors, we nurture our spiritual gifts and call out the spiritual gifts of others. We surrender to the work of sanctification God uses to shape our Christian character. We listen and we share our testimonies. Finally, we commission others to do the same.

It is only appropriate that I close with the testimony of a dear, sweet woman, Mary Kober, who fulfilled all these commitments, and came to this understanding as she served on my mentoring ministry leadership team for over three years:

I have always been a follower.

My husband was a physical therapist in private practice, and I was his self-taught bookkeeper. He was the leader.

When we divorced, I continued on as his bookkeeper and joined a catering business belonging to a friend. She was the cook and leader; I was the bookkeeper and follower.

During this time, I took on four small bookkeeping jobs—for a realtor, a printing company, a bookkeeper, and an attorney—and got my real estate license. In all of these jobs, I was a follower.

By then, I was in my fifties, and when my son and his wife decided to move to North Carolina and take on a new venture, a magazine business, they asked me to be the bookkeeper, and I did. They were the leaders. I was still a follower!

When the magazine was sold and I was 77 years old, I retired. I had never thought about being a leader. I was very happy being a follower.

During the time I was working, I was in Bible Study Fellowship for nine years. Since I was born and brought up Catholic, I had always had a yearning for the Bible but never owned one. Now, I did every Bible study available, learned from Sunday school, took advantage of every opportunity I could, and I still do.

All of this, and I was still a follower.

Three years ago, I was asked to be a mentor—a leader! This was way out of my comfort zone—not just being a leader but teaching other women about a vision (to grow in truth and to discover their life purpose) and a mission (to teach and train women to know and love the Triune God through the truths of the Holy Bible and prayer so they will know who they are in Christ Jesus, and therefore, love their neighbors as Christ loves them). I really felt mentoring could be a wonderful ministry but with me as a follower—someone to learn, not to teach.

Now, in my third year as a mentor, I realize teaching and leading is far more valuable to me than following.

Mary's life embodies what it means to grow, persevere, and find purpose through intentional discipleship. We see God at work in her story, and we are encouraged to cast aside our own fears. No matter what you have been through, you can know without a shadow of doubt that at every transition, every turn, every disappointment, and every new adventure, God was present, shaping your character, strengthening your faith, and preparing you for such a time as now. God loves you.

For every woman who thinks she is not "gifted" or cannot possibly be a leader, Mary's testimony lets them know it is never too late to learn. It is never too late to get started. You, too, can walk in this love. You, too, can mentor for life.

Mentor for Life

1. Are you aware of your spiritual gifts? Consider: What are you passionate about? What are you good at?

2. Ask four or five friends from different seasons of your life, "What are the characteristics you see in me?" What do their responses reveal about your giftedness, calling, and contributions?

3. What questions do you still have about mentoring as intentional discipleship? What more do you need to get started?

4. How do the answers to the previous questions help you better understand your calling, kingdom contributions, or life's purpose? All things considered, what is the best way you can live your life on purpose and mentor to the glory of God?

5. Love Exercise: Write a personal testimony about a time in your life when you were assured of God's love for you. Where were you? How did you know for sure what you were sensing? What did the experience feel like? Who was there? What was your response?

6. Summarize in four or five sentences what you have learned from this chapter.

Tweet This

"ALL Christians are called to the important kingdom work of making disciples." #Mentor4Life @asistasjourney

Afterword

It was nearly 3 p.m. on Wednesday afternoon, the first Wednesday of the month. I'd arrived about five minutes early. Usually, I had to wait a bit, but that was okay with me. I didn't want *him* to be waiting on *me*. He was a busy man with appointments filling the neat boxes of his scheduling calendar. That my name fit in a box on the first Wednesday of every month still surprised me.

Me? Meeting with the president of the seminary? Every month? Each time I walked up to his assistant's desk, I expected to see another name in my place in that box. I was just a girl. Okay, a young woman. But I was still just twenty-four years old. I hadn't even known the meaning of the word "homiletics" when I first enrolled. Now I was a recent grad, still only three years past graduation. Sooo very green in the world of ministry.

Even so, once a month for sixty minutes that sometimes stretched to ninety, for four and a half years, I spent dedicated time with one of the most respected and influential preachers of our day. To be sure, his motivation for this investment of time was about more than me. Unlikely as it seemed, I'd been tapped to represent the seminary on a nationally syndicated radio program five days a week, and this man wisely accepted the responsibility of reviewing my scripts for biblical accuracy, applicable meaning, and effective presentation. As part of his job, he had accepted the responsibility of ensuring my presentations reflected the seminary's mission.

And yet, in addition to making sure I stayed on track and represented the seminary, he also invested in *me*. He spent time tutoring me in biblical interpretation, in speaking techniques, in leadership skills, and in wisdom for everyday life.

He mentored me.

Long after that radio assignment ended, his mentoring continued. When I was offered the presidency of MOPS International, I consulted him for advice. His response? "You need a ministry of your own. This is perfect for your gifts." Who knew? *He did.*

As I prepared sermons and talks for audiences ranging from moms to donors to boards, his teachings echoed in my ears: "Puff the idea. Tell them what you're going to tell them, and then tell them again."

Just a few years ago, I found myself standing in his shadow after joining the team of another national radio ministry, *Discover the Word*. It was the very place he had served for over twenty years.

I've tried to follow his example. I've tried to say "yes" to those needing mentoring from me. I do this in the fulfillment of my job and as an investment in others to help them discover who they are becoming in God's world as they do God's work.

During the two decades I led MOPS International, as much as my schedule would allow, I'd leave my door open and my calendar accessible for mentoring moments, times when someone could stop in for a chat or a laugh or a need for prayer. Sure, in many of those moments, I wondered what I could possibly offer. That old "I'm just a girl" thinking has snared me time and again. I still hear that accusing voice making excuses, telling me to hold back. But I've learned to keep at it, hearing the voices of others encouraging me forward. I believe that just as God used a mentor to make a difference in my life, God might also use me to mentor others.

These days, I work from home, allowing room for coffees and walking buddies and Skype appointments where I prayerfully listen and offer any wisdom that comes to me. At times, the mentoring I offer is formal, with checked boxes and signed forms. At other times, I mentor by informally modeling. In all I do, I invest what I have been given into others, believing that what I have received is what I'm called to share.

Mentoring is for life.

As you've read Natasha's writings on mentoring, I'd love to leave you with a certain "calling" to ponder . . .

What would happen if we intentionally embraced this idea? What if we intentionally sought out people to mentor us, learning from their wisdom and experience? And what if in every role we occupy, we yielded our schedules to those who need what we have to give? What if we awoke every morning asking these questions: What can I learn from others? What can I let others learn from me? Why?

So that more of us look more like Jesus.

Every age.

Every gender.

Every race.

Every country.

Every language.

Every socioeconomic status.

Many years ago, a man invested his time in me, a young woman in the dawn of her ministry, and his investment continues to shape who I am and what I offer to others. Now I am doing the same, investing myself in those around me through intentional mentoring.

Because mentoring is for life.

Elisa Morgan

President Emerita MOPS International, speaker, author, and co-host of *Discover the Word*

Acknowledgments

To Dad, you taught me how to dream big and made me believe I could do anything. I love you always.

To the best godparents a girl could ever ask for, Keith and Linda Jones and James and Joyce Garrett, thanks for making us family and giving us a place to call home.

To my *ezer*-warriors and writing friends: You know who you are. Lesa Engelthaler, God knew exactly what he was doing when he connected us. So glad to be on this journey with you. Carolyn Custis James, thank you for the revelation and truths you speak, for writing prophetically, and for never giving up. Thank you for the encouragement to go to seminary. Dr. Frank James, thank you for the challenge to use my voice and write something every day. To all the Synergy Ezers: Judy Douglass, Jacky Gatliff, Suzie Burden, Pamela Rossi-Keen, Brooke Taylor, and so many others, keep standing, keep fighting, and keep writing.

To the Redbud Writer's Guild: Thanks for providing a community, a reservoir of information, a network, and encouragement through all of my newbie questions.

For all the women of the Women's Mentoring Ministry in Greensboro, North Carolina, including the wonderful women with whom I have had the privilege of serving: my ministry partner Nikki Kober, Melva Walker, Susan Blankenship, Selma Rummage, Debbie Hahn, Mary Kober, Nany Byrd, Carmen Lowery, Lynn Graham, Lea Joyce, Judy Averitte, Charlotte Perkins, Jennifer Byrd, and Katie Long. Without you, there would be no ministry. I am honored for the opportunity I have had to share time and space serving the kingdom alongside you. A special thanks to all who graciously shared their stories and to Pam Carrigan for letting me run with the vision.

To everyone who combed through these chapters and offered critiques and feedback: Nikki Kober, Lindsay Rich, Lesa Engelthaler, Nancy Yoder, Suzanne Burden, Stefini Greer, and Bradley Honeycutt. Summer Ricketts, you were simply the best and most generous in offering your time. For that, I am forever grateful. You have all invested to make this kingdom contribution better.

Special thanks to Brooke Nelson and Mae Cannon for offering encouragement and reviewing the book proposal. Margot Starbuck, you rocked the photo shoot and book proposal! Thanks, girlfriend!

To my *Christianity Today* and *Urban Faith* editors, and my *Gifted for Leadership* editor, Amy Simpson, who has been such a cheerleader, supporter, honest critic, and who has helped me find my voice. Thank you for giving me a writing home.

To the faculty and staff at Gordon-Conwell Theological Seminary (Charlotte, North Carolina), I simply could not have done this project without you. You were gracious and supportive, encouraging and correcting. You provided spiritual formation, wisdom, guidance, and counsel. Dr. Rodney Cooper, thanks for pushing me and giving me the opportunity to use my gifts to the glory of God. Reid Stratterfield, your hopeful words stick to me like glue. You are the most gracious person I have ever known.

To the women who inspired the personal stories on these pages, Mary Thompson, Stefini Greer, and Lilia Ramirez, I love and appreciate you. To the many mentors who have helped me along the way, I know who you are, and I am so thankful for your presence in my life.

To my dear sisters and brothers of Leadership LINKS, Inc., expect great things ahead!

To all my friends, advocates, and ministry partners near and far with whom I have the pleasure of eating, dancing, serving, dreaming, traveling, praying, laughing out loud, and going to the movies, thank you for sharing this life.

To my prayer partner, Suzanne Burden, and my prayer team: May you be rewarded for your labor in this effort and intercession on my behalf. You lift me up.

To my literary agent, Tim Beals! You heard my voice and believed. Thank you! I'm so glad to have your partnership. Here's a toast to many more words ahead.

Thanks to Zondervan for seeing a need for a book like this one, taking a chance on an unpublished author, and standing behind it all the way. I appreciate your patience and support, Ryan Pazdur, Nathan Kroeze, and Harmony Harkema. Grace Claus, you have certainly made this book better!

To all my family members, mentors, and friends who shared in and supported this vision, thank you for your prayers and words of encouragement. I love you and thank God for you.

Ashley girl, it brings my heart great joy to share time and space with you. You are wise, smart, compassionate, funny, and hopeful. I love being your mother.

Deronta, babe, thank you for pressing through, believing God, and making all of this possible. We are better together; let's get stronger together. You are the love of my life.

To my Father God, who am I that you are mindful of me? You alone have done this, and it is marvelous in my sight. You are my master, keep me as your slave. Nothing without you. Captivated by your love.

For His Glory, Natasha

Appendix A

Richard Foster on the Inward Discipline of Study

Note: All content is from the *Celebration of Discipline: The Path to Spiritual Growth.*[1]

> *The purpose of the Spiritual Disciplines is the total transformation of the person. They aim at replacing old destructive habits of thought with new life-giving habits. Nowhere is this purpose more clearly seen than in the discipline of study.*
>
> Richard Foster

The Problems Christians Face

- Bondage to fear and anxiety
- Confusion in the spiritual walk
- Ignorance of the truth
- False teaching

"You will know the truth, and the truth will set you free." John 8:32

The Solution

The Inward Discipline of Study

What is study? "Study is the specific kind of experience in which through careful attention to reality the mind is enabled to move in a certain direction."

The Four Steps of Study

1. Repetition: "Regularly channels the mind in a specific direction, thus ingraining habits of thought."
2. Concentration: "Centers the mind and focuses attention on what is being studied."
3. Comprehension: "Understanding what we are studying" and "Focus on the knowledge of the truth."
4. Reflection: "Defines the significance of what we are studying . . . brings us to see things from God's perspective. In reflection we come to understand not only our subject matter, but ourselves."

Scripture Meditation

Do you not conform any longer to the pattern of this world, but be transformed by the renewing of your mind. Then you will be able to test and approve what God's will is—his good, pleasing and perfect will. (Rom. 12:2)

What the Discipline of Study Requires of the Learner

- Humility: "Study simply cannot happen until we are willing to be subject to the subject matter. We must submit to the system. We must come as student, not teacher. . . . Arrogance and a teachable spirit are mutually exclusive."
- Learn to ask questions.

The Study of Books

For the Mentor: **"To convince people that they must *learn* to study is the major obstacle. Most people assume that because they know how to read words they know how to study."**

Three Rules Govern Our Study of Books

- First Reading: *Understanding* the Book: What is the author saying?
- Second Reading: *Interpreting* the Book: What does the author mean?
- Third Reading: *Evaluating* the Book: Is the author right or wrong?

"Most of us tend to do the third reading right away and often never do the first and second reading at all. We give a critical analysis of the book before we understand what it says. We judge a book to be right or wrong before we interpret its meaning. The wise writer of Ecclesiastes says that there is a time for every matter under heaven, and the time for critical analysis of a book comes *after* careful understanding and interpretation."

The mentoring framework, mentoring resources, and how to carefully understand and interpret a book:

"To read successfully we need the extrinsic aids of *experience, other books, and live discussion.*"

"Experience is the only way we can interpret and relate to what we read."

"Other books can include dictionaries, commentaries, and other interpretative literature, but great books that precede or advance the issue being studied are more significant. Books often have meaning only when they are read in relation to other writings. . . . Great writings that take up the central issues of life interact with one another. They cannot be read in isolation."

Study of the Bible

"In the study of Scripture a high priority is placed upon interpretation: what it means. In the devotional reading of Scripture a high priority is placed upon application: what it means for me. All too often people rush to the application stage and bypass the interpretation stage: they want to know what it means for them before they know what it means!"

Quick Reference: Natasha's Study, "What's in a Bible?" http://asistasjourney.com/2010/10/19/natashas-study-whats-in-a-bible/

Recommended Resources for Bible Study:

How to Read the Bible Book by Book by Gordon D. Fee and Douglas Stuart

How to Read the Bible for All Its Worth by Gordon D. Fee and Douglas Stuart

How to Choose a Translation for All Its Worth by Gordon D. Fee and Mark L. Strauss

The Drama of Scripture: Finding Our Place in the Biblical Story by Craig G. Bartholomew and Michael W. Goheen

Study of Self

"One of the principal objects of our study should be ourselves. We should learn the things that control us . . . *What controls our moods? Why do we like certain people and dislike others? What do these things teach us about ourselves.*"

"Let's learn to ask questions . . . Why do we find it difficult in our culture to have time to develop relationships? Is Western individualism beneficial or destructive? What in our culture is in harmony with the gospel and what is at odds with it? One of the most important functions of Christian prophets in our day is the ability to perceive the consequences of various forces in our culture and to make value judgments upon them."

Appendix B

Mentor: _____

Mentee: _____

Date	Prayer Requests	Accompanying Scripture for Prayer	Date	Answer to Prayer

Appendix C

*Quick Reference Guide for Joining
a Mentoring Group/Ministry*

Q: What is mentoring?

A: Mentoring is a trusted partnership through which one or several persons share wisdom, which fosters spiritual growth that leads to transformed lives of both mentor and mentee(s), as each grows in their love of Jesus Christ, knowledge of self, and love of their neighbors. Entering a mentoring relationship requires mutual commitment of both the mentor and mentee.

Q: What is the purpose of the Mentoring Group/Ministry?

A: The mentoring ministry is an intentional discipleship ministry where women can grow in their Christian faith and personal relationship with God, while building trusted relationships with other like-minded women and learning to love their neighbors as Christ loves them.

> PURPOSE: to disciple women as believers of Christ. "The purpose of mentoring is to transform lives and bring the master's business into focus" (Rom. 8:28–29 and John 15:13–15). The master's kingdom agenda or mission is to build a family of worshippers for himself.
>
> VISION: To mentor women to grow in truth and to discover their life's purpose
>
> MISSION: To teach and train women to *know and love God, know who they are in Christ, and love their neighbors.*

Q: What are the obligations for participating in the ministry?

A: The focus of the ministry is to live out our Christian faith in intimate community with other women. We are mentoring with the intention of knowing God and growing in our love for him, knowing ourselves (who God created us to be and why), and loving others. The result of the ministry is to produce godly women who are focused on cultivating an intimate relationship with God, understand his love for them, and willingly share his love with others.

Effective mentoring is a process that takes time. Women who desire to participate in the ministry agree to the ten-month commitment (gathering once per month) by completing an information form once given the opportunity. Mentees are required to attend all mentoring gatherings and to show up on time. Additionally, there is a small ministry registration fee to cover ministry book resources. Monthly group gatherings will typically last no more than three hours. Participants must commit to preparing for their monthly mentoring group gatherings and cultivating relationships with each other.

Q: What can interested women expect?

A: Participants can expect to be discipled in a safe community of women who love the Lord and commit to a trusting relationship of loving each other well. The call to discipleship is a call to follow Jesus wholeheartedly; it is a call that challenges and transforms. Participants will be taught and trained in the spiritual disciplines and equipped to work for God's kingdom purposes.

Appendix D

Affirmations for Mentoring Groups

1. Actively participate in mentoring group discussions.
2. Focus. Stick to the topic being discussed.
3. Exercise sensitivity to other members of the group. Questions are posed for personal and theological reflection. Listen well. Affirm your sisters whenever possible. Encourage the more hesitant participants.
4. Pray for each other, and pray that you will have an enjoyable and profitable time together.
5. Be cautious about giving opinions and feeling you always need to respond. Do offer wisdom and biblical instruction that is supported by Scripture.
6. Feel free to share your personal experiences. Talk about yourself and your own situation, not the situations of others, which could lead to gossip.
7. Be open. Expect God to teach you through the Scriptures being discussed and through other members of the group.
8. Maintain confidentiality. Anything said in the group is not to be discussed outside the group unless there is an emergency, cause for concern for someone's physical safety, or specific permission is given to do so.

Appendix E

Weekly Time Management Tracker

	Sunday	Monday	Tuesday	Wednesday	Thursday	Friday	Saturday
AM Hours							
5:00–5:30							
5:30–6:00							
6:00–6:30							
6:30–7:00							
7:00–7:30							
7:30–8:00							
8:00–8:30							
8:30–9:00							
9:00–9:30							
9:30–10:00							
10:00–10:30							
10:30–11:00							
11:00–11:30							
11:30–12:00							
PM Hours							
12:00–12:30							

12:30–1:00						
1:00–1:30						
1:30–2:00						
2:00–2:30						
2:30–3:00						
3:00–3:30						
3:30–4:00						
4:00–4:30						
4:30–5:00						
5:00–5:30						
5:30–6:00						
6:00–6:30						
6:30–7:00						
7:00–7:30						
7:30–8:00						
8:00–8:30						
8:30–9:00						
9:00–9:30						
9:30–10:00						
10:00–10:30						
10:30–11:00						
11:00–11:30						
11:30–12:00 midnight						

End-of-Week Evaluation:

1. How many hours were devoted to sleep (per night)?
2. How many hours were devoted to study?
3. How many hours were devoted to exercise?
4. How many hours were devoted to leisure?
5. How many hours were devoted to cultivating healthy relationships with family and friends?
6. How many hours were devoted to work?
7. How many hours were devoted to volunteer work or service commitments?

Personal Reflection:

1. How are you being a good steward of the time God has given you?
2. Do you need to make adjustments? If so, where and how? Who will hold you accountable to these changes?

Share these results, evaluations, and reflections with trusted friends.

Appendix F

Sample Mentoring Information Sign-up Form

Name _____

Mailing Address _____

City _____ State _____ Zip Code _____

Email Address _____

Primary Phone _____ Secondary Phone _____

Age: __ 18–21 __ 22–30 __ 31–40 __ 41–50 __ 51–60 __ 61-above

Single ____ Married ____ Widowed ____

Children? ____ Yes ____ No # of Children: ____

    Ages of Children: _____

____ Employed Full/Part-time

    Where: _____

____ Volunteer

    Where: _____

____ Retired

    From where: _____

____ Student

    Where: _____

Are you a Christian? __ Yes __ No __ Not sure

    If yes, how long? _____

Are you a member of a church? __ Yes __ No

    Where? _____

Are you serving in a ministry? __ Yes __ No

What is the capacity of your service and where:

_____

Are you willing to commit to the mentoring ministry?

__ Yes __ Undecided

What are your expectations of the mentoring ministry?

_____

What other information would you like to share with our leadership team? _____

Note: All information provided on this form will be used for the sole purpose of group placement. Information will not be shared without permission.

Mentoring groups will meet once a month at the following times. Group gathering dates will be confirmed by the entire group during the first mentoring session.

Please prioritize your top 3 meeting time preferences below with #1 being your first option.

	Day/Time/Location
	Monday, 6:00–9:00 PM, Georgetown 10285
	Monday, 6:15–9:15 PM, New Haven 10264
	Monday, 6:30–9:30 PM, Greenville 10418
	Tuesday, 6:00–9:00 PM, Georgetown 10286
	Tuesday, 6:00–9:00 PM, Goldenfield 10359
	Tuesday, 6:00–9:00 PM, Greenville 10418
	Wednesday, 9:30 AM–12:30 PM, Greenville 10453
	Thursday, 6:00–9:00 PM, Greenville 10453
	Thursday, 6:30–9:30 PM, Greenville 10418
	Saturday, 9:00 AM–12 PM, Greenville 10418

Notes

Part 1: The Mentoring Call to Action

1. Halee Gray Scott, *Dare Mighty Things: Mapping the Challenges of Leadership for Christian Women* (Grand Rapids, MI: Zondervan, 2014), 122.

Chapter 1: Join the Mission

1. Leighton Ford, *Transforming Leadership: Jesus' Way of Creating Vision, Shaping Values, and Empowering Change* (Downers Grove, IL: InterVarsity, 1991), 22.
2. Dietrich Bonhoeffer, *The Cost of Discipleship* (New York: Touchstone, 1959), 38.
3. Merriam-Webster, *Merriam-Webster's Collegiate Dictionary*, 10th ed. (Springfield, MA: Merriam-Webster, 1996), 726.
4. "1 a friend of Odysseus entrusted with the education of Odysseus's son Telemachus" (Merriam-Webster, *Merriam-Webster's Collegiate Dictionary*, 726.)
5. Regi Campbell, *Mentor Like Jesus* (Nashville: Broadman and Holman, 2009), 18.
6. *Mentee* is the word used throughout this resource to refer to the person being mentored. Some resources also use *mentoree* to define this person.
7. This passage includes three instructions or commands: make disciples, baptise, and teach. Mentoring focuses on the first and third instructions, while the Protestant church generally understands baptism as a sacrament regularly administered by officiates of the local church.
8. Matt. 22:37–39; Mark 12:30–31; Luke 10:27; Deut. 6:5; Lev. 19:18.
9. Paul D. Borden, *Direct Hit* (Nashville: Abingdon, 2006), 19.
10. Psalm 86; Isa. 60:21; Rom. 11:36; 1 Cor. 6:20, 31; Rev. 4:11.
11. Ps. 16:5–11; Ps. 144:15; Isa. 12:2; Luke 2:10; Rev. 21:3–4; Phil. 4:4.
12. The General Assembly at Augusta, Georgia, December 1861, with Revised Proof Texts adopted by the General Assemby of 1910, with amendments that were enacted by the General Assemblies of 1886, 1939, 1942, and 1944, *The Confession of Faith of the Presbyterian Church in the United States Together with the Larger Catechism and the Shorter Catechism* (Richmond, VA: John Knox, 1952), 387. Also available online by the Assembly of Divines at Westminister at Edinburgh,

July 28, 1648, "The Westminster Shorter Catechism," Puritan Seminary, http://puritanseminary.org/wp-content/uploads/2012/04/Shorter_Catechism.pdf (accessed August 27, 2012).

13. Ps. 100:1–3.

14. Matt. 6:10; Ps. 72:19; Isa. 6:3.

15. Tony Evans, *Oneness Embraced through the Eyes of Tony Evans: A Fresh Look at Reconciliation, the Kingdom, and Justice* (Chicago: Moody, 2011), 243.

16. Darlene Zschech, *The Art of Mentoring: Embracing the Great Generational Transition* (Minneapolis: Bethany, 2011), 12.

17. The Lausanne Congress, "Reflections of the Lausanne Theology Working Group," Lausanne Movement, http://www.lausanne.org/content/twg-three-wholes (accessed September 16, 2015).

18. Eph. 2:9–10; 4:11–16.

Chapter 2: Connect Evangelism and Discipleship

1. Brenda Salter McNeil, *A Credible Witness: Reflections on Power, Evangelism, and Race* (Downers Grove, IL: InterVarsity, 2008), 21.

2. Consider 1 Cor. 9:19–23.

3. The word *evangelical* "[comes] out of the Greek word *euangelion*," "good news," or "gospel." In its most general sense *evangelical* means being characterized by a concern for the essential core of the Christian message, which proclaims the possibility of salvation through the person and work of Jesus Christ. More specifically, *evangelicalism* . . . emphasizes the need to experience personal conversion through belief in Christ and his work on the cross, and commitment to the authority of Scripture as the infallible guide for Christian faith and practice."
   Stanley J. Grenz, David Guretzki, and Cherith Fee Nordling, *Pocket Dictionary of Theological Terms* (Downers Grove, IL: InterVarsity, 1999), 47–48.

4. John 14:6–13; Matt. 1:23.

5. Compare John 1:35–51 with what we have come to know as the Evangelism Movement.

6. McNeil, *A Credible Witness*, 74–75.

7. Matt. 8:18–22; 10:37–42; Luke 9:57–62; 14:25–35.

8. Robert E. Coleman, *The Master Plan of Evangelism*, 2nd ed. (Grand Rapids, MI: Revell, 2010), 48–49, emphasis mine.

9. Ibid., 49.

10. Pastor Wesley was interviewed for an academic study and blog series on racial reconciliation. The interview can be found at Natasha Sistrunk Robinson, "#RacialRec: Raising the Voice of the Black Preacher ~ Rev. Dr. Howard-John Wesley Part II," *A Sista's Journey* blog at WordPress.com, http://goo.gl/chIjbc (accessed December 18, 2012).

11. Matt. 14:13–16; Mark 6:30–37; Luke 9:10–15; John 6:1–6.

12. Luke 8:2–46.
13. 1 Corinthians 13.

Chapter 3: Shape Culture and the Church

1. Richard J. Foster, *Celebration of Discipline: The Path to Spiritual Growth* (San Francisco: HarperOne, 1998), 75–76.
2. David Platt. *Radical: Taking Back Your Faith from the American Dream* (Colorado Springs: Multnomah, 2010), 46.
3. Natasha Sistrunk Robinson, "#RacialRec: American Slavery, Neglected Voices, and History of the Church," *A Sista's Journey* blog at WordPress .com, http://goo.gl/D7vKRX (accessed December 20, 2012).
4. Andy Crouch, *Culture Making: Recovering Our Creative Calling* (Downers Grove, IL: InterVarsity, 2008), 68.
5. Ibid.
6. Ibid, 69.
7. Ibid, 70.
8. Ibid, 67.
9. Platt, *Radical*, 111, 61–64, 122, 164–65.
10. Janet O. Hagberg and Robert A. Guelich, *The Critical Journey: Stages in the Life of Faith*, 2nd ed. (Salem, WI: Sheffield, 2005), 82–83.
11. Platt, *Radical*, 50.
12. Thomas Penny, "U.S. White Population Will Be Minority by 2042, Government Says," Bloomberg, http://goo.gl/JO9AQ3 (accessed August 14, 2012).
13. George Cladis, *Leading the Team-Based Church: How Pastors and Church Staff Can Grow Together into a Powerful Fellowship of Leaders* (San Francisco: Jossey-Bass, 1999), 64.
14. Robert P. Jones, "Why Are Millennials Leaving the Church?" *Washington Post,* http://goo.gl/SLJrXS (accessed August 14, 2012). Also read: Rachel Held Evans, "Why Millennials Are Leaving the Church," CNN Belief Blog, http://goo.gl/xMeHXp (accessed September 5, 2013). There are some who believe that this mass exodus is more of a cultural problem in the white evangelical churches. Sample Reference: Bryant T. Calvin, "Why Aren't Black Millennials Leaving the Church," *Relevant Magazine*, http://goo.gl/c37EfW (accessed September 5, 2013).
15. Wendy Griffith, "Know Your Bible? Many Christians Don't," Christian Broadcasting Network, http://goo.gl/BRQ8Zd (accessed December 21, 2012).
16. Dr. Rodney Cooper, Kenneth and Jean Hansen Professor of Discipleship and Leadership Development, lectured that churches rarely split over theological convictions. Most often, they split, wither,

or die as a result of poor leadership. This principle is echoed in the following resources:

Alfred Poirier, *The Peace Making Pastor: A Biblical Guide to Resolving Church Conflict* (Grand Rapids, MI: Baker, 2006).

Ron Susek, *Firestorm: Preventing and Overcoming Church Conflicts* (Grand Rapids, MI: Baker, 1999).

17. Author Carolyn Custis James has written extensively on this topic. Her most recent book, *Half the Church: Recapturing God's Global Vision for Women*, is an excellent resource for further research.

18. On the topic of racial reconciliation, diversity and the church, see CNN's article, "Why Many Americans Prefer Their Sundays Segregated," http://www.cnn.com/2008/LIVING/wayoflife/08/04/segregated.sundays/index.html (accessed November 2, 2012); Scott Williams's book, *Church Diversity: Sunday The Most Segregated Day of the Week*; Christena Cleveland's book, *Disunity in Christ: Uncovering the Hidden Forces That Keep Us Apart*; and my blog series on racial reconciliation: http://asistasjourney.com/2012/12/14/racial-reconciliation-racialrec-series-summary-2012/ (accessed December 14, 2012).

19. View *Campaign for a Cause* video at http://www.onedayswages.org/ (accessed September 5, 2013).

Additional facts and resources are available at 58: Fast. Forward. The End to Poverty. www.live58.org (accessed September 5, 2013).

Chapter 4: Multiply the Kingdom and the Priesthood

1. George Barna, *Think Like Jesus: Make the Right Decision Every Time* (Nashville: Integrity, 2003), 134–35. Scripture references: Rom. 7:8–25; 1 Peter 5:8.
2. United States Naval Academy: Annapolis, *Reef Points 1998–1999: The Annual Handbook of the Brigade of Midshipmen*, 93rd ed., 119.
3. Tony Evans, *The Kingdom Agenda: What a Way to Live* (Chicago: Moody, 2006), 27.
4. Matt. 2:20–23.
5. Num. 18:7; Isa. 61:6; Ex. 19:5–6; 1 Peter 2:5, 9.
6. Rev. 1:5–6; also see Rev. 5:10.
7. Crouch, *Culture Making*, 76.

Part II: The Mentoring Commitment

1. John 12:40; Acts 2:37; 15:8–9; 16:14; 2 Thess. 3:5; 2 Cor. 1:21–22; 3:2–3; Eph. 3:17; Rom. 2:29; 8:26–27; Heb. 8:10.
2. Eph. 4:22–24; Rom. 12:2.
3. Col. 2:2–3.

Mentoring: A Commitment to Presence

1. Henri J. M. Nouwen, *In the Name of Jesus: Reflections on Christian Leadership* (New York: Crossroad, 1992), 61.

Chapter 5: Presence with God

1. Ruth Haley Barton, *Invitation to Solitude and Silence: Experiencing God's Transforming Presence* (Downers Grove, IL: InterVarsity, 2004), 20.
2. Henri Nouwen, *The Way of the Heart: The Spirituality of the Desert Fathers and Mothers* (San Francisco: HarperOne: 1981), 27.
3. Crouch, *Culture Making*, 67–73.
4. In addition to Scripture, this exercise is inspired by Regi Campbell's *Mentor Like Jesus* (103–8).
5. Mark 1:35; Matt. 26:36; Luke 5:26; 6:12.
6. Matt. 26:36–38; Mark 14:32–34.

Chapter 6: Presence with Others

1. Robert J. Wicks, *Sharing Wisdom: The Practical Art of Giving and Receiving Mentoring* (New York: Crossroad, 2000), 41.
2. Nouwen, *The Way of the Heart*, 28.
3. Ibid., 30.
4. Gen. 1:26–27; 2:23.
5. Gathering with their group monthly allows mentors an opportunity to have their training with the mentoring leadership team early in the month, and gives mentors adequate preparation time for their mentoring group gathering. A monthly gathering option also gives mentors the opportunity (if they desire) to consider other connection points for their mentoring group, either through Bible study, community service, fellowship meals, or exploring life and hobbies together.
   At first glance, three hours seems like a long time commitment. It is actually a much smaller obligation that those who have weekly Bible study or small group commitments. Three hours allows for a focused, unrushed, learning, sharing, and practical application within the group. Mentors on the leadership team have often been surprised by how quickly the time passes.
6. Unlike traditional small groups or evangelistic efforts, no "guests" are invited in to visit the mentoring group gatherings.
7. Nouwen, *Way of the Heart*, 27.
8. This learning tool is adopted from Campbell, *Mentor Like Jesus*, 74.
9. A. W. Tozer, *The Knowledge of the Holy* (New York: HarperCollins, 1961), 1.
10. Foster, *Celebration of Discipline*, 64–66.

Mentoring: A Commitment to a Disciplined Life

1. Diane J. Chandler, *Christian Spiritual Formation: An Integrated Approach for Personal and Relational Wholeness* (Downers Grove, IL: InterVarsity, 2014), 79.

Chapter 7: Discipleship

1. James W. Sire, *Discipleship of the Mind: Learning to Love God in the Ways We Think* (Downers Grove, IL: InterVarsity, 1990), 98.
2. Matt. 22:37, emphasis added. Also see Luke 10:27.
3. This has been the slogan for the United Negro College Fund for more than three decades.
4. Valeria Andrews, Whoopi Godbert, Kevin Cloud, and Roni Skies, "Pay Attention," lyric from *The Sister Act 2* soundtrack, 1993.
5. Recommended reading: John Stott, *The Radical Disciple: Some Neglected Aspects of Our Calling* (Downers Grove, IL: InterVarsity, 2010).
6. Eddie Byun, *Justice Awakening: How You and Your Church Can Help End Human Trafficking* (Downers Grove, IL: InterVarsity, 2014), 27.
7. "The word theology is derived from two Greek words, *theos* and *logos*, meaning reflection or discourse about God. Christian theology is essentially a compilation of our most fundamental beliefs." Bruce Demarest and Keith J. Matthews, eds., *Dictionary of Everyday Theology and Culture* (Colorado Spring: NavPress, 2010), 414–15.
8. Carolyn Custis James, *When Life and Beliefs Collide: How Knowing God Makes a Difference* (Grand Rapids, MI: Zondervan, 2001), 233.
9. John 14:15; 14:23, 15:10; 1 John 2:3; 5:2–3.
10. Howard W. Stone and James O. Duke, *How to Think Theologically*, 2nd ed. (Minneapolis: Fortress, 2006), 83.
11. Of course this state of depravity does not change the fact that we are all created in God's image. Human beings have value because we are made by God, and as part of his creation, our existence pleases him. But the Holy Spirit gives us the desire to do something we are currently incapable of doing on our own, to live as God originally intended: in love with Him; with humble responsibility for creation and in unity with other human beings.
12. Kenneth S. Kantzer, "A Systematic Biblical Dogmatics: What Is It and How Is It to Be Done?" in *Doing Theology in Today's World: Essays in Honor of Kenneth S. Kantzer*, ed. John D. Woodbridge and Thomas Edward McComiskey (Grand Rapids, MI: Zondervan, 1991), 467.
13. John 8:31–32, emphasis mine.
14. Arnold Cole and Pamela Caudill Ovwigho, "Understanding the Bible Engagement Challenge: Scientific Evidence for the Power of 4" (Research Report), Center for Bible Engagement, www.c4be.org, December 2009, 2.

15. Ibid., 3–4.
16. Ibid., 5.
17. Ibid., 6.
18. Ibid., 6–7. "While these findings are truly impressive, it is important to note that they are based on research with a select sample—namely 8,665 self-identified Christian adults who were willing to participate in an online survey about Bible engagement."
19. Ibid., 12.
20. Reference the "Mentoring Resources" section at the back of the book.

Chapter 8: Discipleship of the Soul

1. Michael Card, *Scribbling in the Sand Study Guide: Christ and Creativity* (Downers Grove, IL: InterVarsity, 2002), 103.
2. Peter Scazzero, *Emotionally Healthy Spirituality: Unleash a Revolution in Your Life in Christ* (Nashville: Thomas Nelson, 2006), 128.
3. Prayer resources are included under "Solitude, Silence, and Prayer" in the "Further Reading" section of this book.
4. Luke 11:1.
5. We are responsible for checking the motives of our prayers: James 4:3–10.
6. Foster, *Celebration of Discipline*, 33.
7. Ps. 91:14–16; 116:1–2; 118: 5–7, and countless other Psalms. Also see Matt. 7:7–11 and 1 John 5:14–15.
8. Tony Evans, *Tony Evans Speaks Out on Fasting* (Chicago: Moody, 2000), 7.
9. Note: It is recommended that a person starts fasting progressively, beginning by skipping one meal and building stamina from there. For medical reasons, not all people should fast, and if there are medical concerns, please consult with your physician. Scot McKnight addresses medical concerns in his book *Fasting* and draws attention to two medical resources: Lee Goldman and Dennis Ausiello, eds., *Cecil Textbook of Medicine*, 22nd ed. (Philadelphia: Saunders, 2004) and Jerrold B. Leikin and Martin S. Lipsky, eds., *American Medical Association Complete Medical Encyclopedia* (New York: Random House Reference, 2003).
10. Acts 19:9–19; 3:2–3; 14:23.
11. Matt. 4:1–4; Luke 4:1–4; Acts 9:1–11.
12. Matt. 9:15; Mark 2:20; Luke 5:35.
13. Foster, *Celebration of Discipline*, 52. The foundation of which is firmly established in Isaiah 58.
14. Scot McKnight, *Fasting* (Nashville: Thomas Nelson, 2009), xxi.
15. Ibid., xiv.
16. Evans, *Tony Evans Speaks Out on Fasting*, 6–7.

17. As mentors, fasting is not something we should fear or shy away from simply because we have not done it before. You can teach and practice this discipline with your mentees, and it can be a powerful experience for you and for them.

18. Evans, *Tony Evans Speaks Out on Fasting*, 12.

19. Foster, *Celebration of Discipline*, 75.

20. Helen Cepero, *Journaling as a Spiritual Practice: Encountering God through Attentive Writing* (Downers Grove, IL: InterVarsity, 2008), 20.

21. Foster, *Celebration of Discipline*, 70.

22. Ps. 119:9, 11; 2 Tim. 3:16–17.

23. This instruction for prayer was adopted from Regi Campbell's *Mentor Like Jesus*, chapter 7.

24. Prayer Log sample is available in Appendix B.

25. Read Scriptures Matt. 22:37–40 and (sit at the feet of Jesus) Luke 10:39–42.

26. Foster, *Celebration of Discipline*, 75.

Mentoring: A Commitment to God's Mission

1. Charles Van Engen, *Mission on the Way: Issues in Mission Theology* (Grand Rapids, MI: Baker, 1996), 26–27.

Chapter 9: Mission Accomplishment

1. Coleman, *Master Plan of Evangelism*, 2nd ed., 38.

2. Also see 1 Tim. 4:7–10.

3. This passage is not about works-based salvation. In this passage, Paul mentions obtaining a crown. In others, he references treasures and rewards that we receive in heaven for the work that we do on earth. So the work does not save us. God alone does that. However, the Bible is clear that children of God will be rewarded for their earthly acts of obedience when they get to heaven.

4. Evans, *The Kingdom Agenda*, 113–14.

5. James 1:2–4; Rom. 5:1–4.

6. Campbell, *Mentor Like Jesus*, 120.

7. The apostle James writes about true faith which compels us to right action (James 2:14-26). The apostle John paints a beautiful picture of what it means to live in light of God's light and the freedom from sin which Christ offers (1 John 1:5–2:6; 3:4–10). In light of Christ, the apostle Paul calls believers to live as people of righteousness, and not abuse the grace of God (Romans 6).

8. Dietrich Bonhooffer, *The Cost of Discipleship* (New York: Simon and Schuster, 1959), 43–45.

9. Ibid, 37.

10. Campbell, *Mentor Like Jesus*, 18, 132–33.

Chapter 10: Rally the Troops

1. Dr. Carson Pue, *Mentoring Wisdom: Living and Leading Well* (Ontario, Canada: Castle Quay Books, 2011), 61.
2. Recommended Reading: Dallas Willard, "Spiritual Formation in Christ: A Perspective on What It Is and How It Might Be Done," http://www.dwillard.org/articles/artview.asp?artID=81 (accessed September 6, 2014).
3. Scazzero, *Emotionally Healthy Spirituality*, 18.
4. There may be women who need professional help for various reasons, and if needed, they should absolutely get professional help. On the other hand, it's more common that the women who come for mentoring are isolated and in need of TLC (Tender Loving Care). They simply want someone who cares enough to *stop, be present*, and listen. They need a reminder concerning their identity in Christ, and they need someone to show them that they are loved.
5. For a sample of the speaking points provided to our mentors to assist in sharing the ministry's message, see Appendix C.
6. Campbell, *Mentor Like Jesus*, 130.
7. A sample of mentoring group affirmations can be found in Appendix D.
8. Small group ministry is a very specific ministry and culture within the church. Many times, small group ministries are evangelistic in their approach by: (a) always inviting new people into small group gatherings, (b) sometimes specializing by the way people are grouped together (e.g., youth, young couples, moms, widows, college students, etc.), and (c) intentionally splitting or multiplying the small groups. The mentoring ministry, however, is not "evangelistic" or structured in that way. The mentoring ministry bridges the gap between evangelism and discipleship with the goal of intentionally investing more focused time with a small group of people and raising up disciples who live their lives on purpose for God. Multiplication occurs as mentees grow in maturity, complete mentoring training themselves, and become able teachers who lead new mentoring groups. Multiplication also occurs as mentors and mentees become clearer about their life's work and ministry, and go into the world with a new passion for intentionally discipling others where they already work and live. Once established, mentoring groups are not split up for the purpose of multiplying. In these ways, the foundation, purpose, and structure of the mentoring ministry may be unique from your traditional understanding of small group ministry. If the reader approaches this section using the context of a small group ministry, the content might be somewhat confusing. It would be best to take this information at face value exactly as it is presented in the book and not think of mentoring as a small group ministry.

9. Larry Osborne, *Leadership Journal*, Christianity Today, Spring 2009, 13, http://christianitytoday.imirus.com/Mpowered/book/vls09/i2/p12 (accessed September 6, 2014).
10. If they continually made annual commitments, mentees in our ministry context would generally stay in the same mentoring group for three years before they were commissioned for specific service in the Lord's kingdom.
11. This gives mentors an opportunity to have their monthly leadership training and soul care with the mentoring leadership team and allows adequate preparation time for the mentoring group gathering.
12. Matt. 22:36–39; 28:19–20; Mark 12:28–31; Luke 10:25–28.
13. See Time Management handout in Appendix E.

Mentoring: A Commitment to Community

1. Gilbert Bilezikian, *Community 101: Reclaiming the Local Church as Community of Oneness* (Grand Rapids, MI: Zondervan, 1997), 33, 35.

Chapter 11: Be Your Sister's or Brother's Keeper

1. The names in this story have been changed.
2. View Sherry Turkle Ted Talk: Connected, but Alone? Read articles: https://medium.com/tech-talk/c663; http://www.connect-world.com/; http://pacificcrossroads.org/; and http://www.theatlan.
3. Anita Lustrea is Moody's *Midday Connection* former broadcast host and author of *What Women Tell Me*.
4. FullFill Weekly Blog: http://fullfillmagazine.blogspot.com/2012/04/what-women-tell-me-need-for-connecting.html (accessed April 30, 2012).
5. Henry Cloud and John Townsend, *Safe People: How to Find Relationship That Are Good for You and Avoid Those That Aren't* (Grand Rapids, MI: Zondervan, 1995), 143.
6. Janet O. Hagberg and Robert A. Guelich, *The Critical Journey: Stages in the Life of Faith* (Salem, WI: Sheffield, 1973), 181.
7. Mic. 6:4.
8. Ex. 17:8–16; 24:13; 33:11; Num. 11:28; 27:18–23.
9. Carolyn Custis James, *Maelstrom: Manhood Swept into the Currents of a Changing World* (Grand Rapids, MI: Zondervan, 2015), chapter 15.
10. 1 Cor. 7:1–9, 28–35; 9:1–6.
11. Consider the IF:Table gathering. They offer a monthly recipe and four questions to discuss over dinner. I use this tool monthly with a group of millennial women, and they love it! IF:Table, https://ifgathering.com/table/.

Chapter 12: This Makes a Family

1. Mark 3:30–21; John 7:1–5.
2. *Eros, storge, philia,* and *agape* are all ancient Greek words that are translated to mean "love" in our English text. *Storge* defines the type of love a parent would have toward a child or vice versa. *Philia* is a love or affection that one has toward a sibling or friend. It is where we get the word, Philadelphia, the city of brotherly love.
3. John 14:15, 23. Note his own obedience in John 14:31.
4. Robert J. Wicks, *Touching the Holy: Ordinariness, Self-Esteem, and Friendship* (Notre Dame, IN: Sorin, 2007), 117–23.
5. Ibid., 124. Also see pages 123–29.
6. Ibid., 123–29.
7. Ibid., 129–30, 132.
8. Ibid., 132.
9. Ibid., 133.
10. Ibid., 144.
11. Ibid., 132–50.
12. Careful considerations is made if a woman or someone she loves is in danger or in need of professional assistance that must be provided outside of the group. Even these extreme cases are responded to with caution, care, and the knowledge of the mentor involved. We tread with wisdom and discernment for the purpose of providing help in the form of safety, healing, reconciliation, and/or peacemaking, and not hurting the mentee or others involved.
13. Cloud and Townsend, *Safe People*, 143.
14. Ibid., 171–72.

Mentoring: A Commitment to Relationships

1. Mark Labberton, *The Dangerous Act of Loving Your Neighbor: Seeing Others through the Eyes of Jesus* (Downers Grove, IL: InterVarsity, 2010), 170.

Chapter 13: Embrace Unity in Diversity

1. Zschech, *The Art of Mentoring*, 138.
2. Natasha Sistrunk Robinson, "Why I Don't Want My Child to Be 'Colorblind'," *Christianity Today*, http://goo.gl/5uSvLk (accessed August 27, 2014).
3. Labberton, *Dangerous Act*, 74–75.
4. Christena Cleveland, *Disunity in Christ: Uncovering the Hidden Forces That Keep Us Apart* (Downers Grove, IL: InterVarsity, 2013), 39.
5. Paul David Tripp, *What Did You Expect? Redeeming the Realities of Marriage* (Wheaton, IL: Crossway, 2010), 209.
6. Ibid., 211.

7. "Your Story, My Story" is a website dedicated to sharing stories. One of the themes features stories of those who have been rejected by the church, http://www.yourstorymystory.com/featured-articles/rejected-by-church/ (accessed September 10, 2013).

8. Cleveland, *Disunity in Christ*, 95.

9. This phrase is referenced from Dr. Brenda Salter McNeil's book *A Credible Witness: Reflections on Power, Evangelism, and Race.*

10. Cleveland, *Disunity in Christ*, 31.

Chapter 14: Embrace All Women

1. James, *Half the Church*, 48.

2. Gen. 1:26–31; Ps. 139:13–16; Phil. 2:13.

3. Eph. 2:10; Jer. 1:5; Acts 9:15.

4. In John 4:18, Jesus tells us that this woman had five husbands and was in a relationship with a man who was not her husband. We do not know if this woman had been a widow several times over. However, context leads the reader to believe that it is likely according to Matthew 5:31–32 that she had either been in adulterous relationship(s) or was currently in an adulterous relationship. She was drawing water from the well at the time of day which allowed her to avoid the other women in what was normally a social and communal time. For whatever reason, this was a woman to be avoided. When Jesus revealed himself to her as Messiah, she ran into the town and said, "Come, see a man who told me everything I ever did" (John 4:29). Clearly, she knew the perceptions of her and because of her encounter with Jesus, she was free from all guilt and shame.

5. Ex. 3:6; Matt. 22:32.

6. Sample Mentoring Information Form is provided in Appendix F. This form is provided courtesy of ministry team leaders Selma Rummage, Susan Blankenship, and Nancy Byrd.

Mentoring: A Commitment to Love

1. Idelette McVicker, "Manifesto: Let us be Women who Love," *SheLoves Magazine*, http://shelovesmagazine.com/manifesto/ (accessed October 6, 2015).

Chapter 15: Obedience and Sacrifice

1. John 15:13.

2. In addition to verse 10, John 14:15, 23 and 1 John 2:3, 5:2–4 also reveal these truths.

3. John 14:14, 23; 15:10; 1 John 2:3; 5:2–3.

4. In this passage, bearing fruit is a metaphor that reveals the outward

results that reflect an inward change. Reference: Matt. 7:15–20; Luke 6:43–45.
5. God calls us to persevere in our faith.
6. 1 Corinthians 13.
7. Natasha Sistrunk Robinson, "When You Learn, Teach," *SheLoves Magazine*, http://shelovesmagazine.com/2014/learn-teach/ (accessed June 12, 2015).
8. Heb. 5:11–14.

Chapter 16: Spiritual Gifts and Christian Character

1. Robertson McQuilkin, *Life in the Spirit* (Nashville: Lifeway, 1997), 144.
2. James 4:2.
3. "Sanctification" simply means to be set apart for a particular purpose. It is an immediate and gracious act of God to make us holy or righteous before him, and the continuous act or work of God to keep us set apart for his good purposes.

Appendix A

1. Foster, *Celebration of Discipline*, chapter 5: "The Discipline of Study."

Additional Resources for Further Reading

Go deeper in studying the mentoring principles presented in this book by considering this topical and alphabetical list. This is not an exhaustive list. It includes resources that have personally benefited my faith and mentoring journey.

Evangelism

Coleman, Robert E. *The Master Plan of Evangelism*, 2nd Ed. Grand Rapids, MI: Revell, 2010.

Rah, Soong-Chan. *The Next Evangelicalism: Freeing the Church from Western Cultural Captivity*. Downers Grove, IL: InterVarsity, 2009.

McNeil, Brenda Salter. *A Credible Witness: Reflections on Power, Evangelism and Race*. Downers Grove, IL: InterVarsity, 2008.

Bible Reading and Study

Bartholomew, Craig G., and Michael W. Goheen. *The Drama of Scripture: Finding Our Place in the Biblical Story*. Grand Rapids, MI: Baker Academic, 2004.

Fee, Gordon D. and Douglas Stuart. *How to Read the Bible Book by Book*. Grand Rapids, MI: Zondervan, 2002.

Fee, Gordon D. and Douglas Stuart. *How to Read the Bible for All It's Worth*, 3rd Ed. Grand Rapids, MI: Zondervan, 2003.

Roberts, Vaughan. *God's Big Picture: Tracing the Storyline of the Bible*. Downers Grove, IL: InterVarsity, 2002.

Discipleship of the Soul

Hagberg, Janet O., and Robert A. Guelich. *The Critical Journey: Stages in the Life of Faith*, 2nd Ed. Salem, WI: Sheffield, 2005.

Macchia, Stephen A. *Crafting a Rule of Life: An Invitation to the Well-Ordered Way*. Downers Grove, IL: InterVarsity, 2012.

Scazzero, Peter. *Emotionally Healthy Spirituality: Unleash a Revolution in Your Life in Christ*. Nashville: Thomas Nelson, 2006.

Fasting

Evans, Tony. *Tony Evans Speaks Out on Fasting*. Chicago: Moody, 2000.

McKnight, Scot. *Fasting*. Nashville: Thomas Nelson, 2009.

Piper, John. *A Hunger for God: Desiring God through Fasting and Prayer*. Wheaton, IL: Crossway, 1997.

Journaling

Cepero, Helen. *Journaling as a Spiritual Practice: Encountering God through Attentive Writing*. Downers Grove, IL: InterVarsity, 2008.

Kent, Keri Wyatt. *Deeply Loved: 40 Ways in 40 Days to Experience the Heart of Jesus*. Nashville: Abington, 2012.

Relationship Building in the Church

Cloud, Henry, and John Townsend. *Safe People: How to Find Relationships That Are Good for You and Avoid Those That Aren't*. Grand Rapids, MI: Zondervan, 1995.

Labberton, Mark. *The Dangerous Act of Loving Your Neighbor: Seeing Others through the Eyes of Jesus*. Downers Grove, IL: InterVarsity, 2010.

Sande, Ken. *The Peacemaker: A Biblical Guide to Resolving Personal Conflict*. Grand Rapids, MI: Baker, 2004.

Wicks, Robert J. *Touching the Holy: Ordinariness, Self-Esteem, and Friendship*. Notre Dame, IN: Sorin, 2007.

Spiritual Disciplines and Spiritual Formation

Foster, Richard J. *Celebration of Discipline: The Path to Spiritual Growth*. San Francisco: HarperOne, 1998.

Nouwen, Henri J.M. *In the Name of Jesus: Reflection on Christian Leadership*. New York: Crossroad, 1989.

Spiritual Gifts

McQuilkin, Robertson. *Life in the Spirit*. Nashville: Lifeway, 2003.

Solitude, Silence, and Prayer

Barton, Ruth Haley. *Invitation to Solitude and Silence: Experiencing God's Transforming Presence*. Downers Grove, IL: InterVarsity, 2004.

Nouwen, Henri, *The Way of the Heart: The Spirituality of the Desert Fathers and Mothers*. San Francisco: HarperOne, 1981.

Theological Reflection and Discipleship of the Mind

Adler, Mortimer J. and Charles Van Doren. *How to Read a Book: The Classic Guide to Intelligent Reading*. New York: Simon and Schuster, 1972.

Barna, George. *Think Like Jesus: Make the Right Decision Every Time*. Nashville: Integrity, 2003.

Demarest, Bruce, and Keith J. Matthews, eds. *Dictionary of Everyday Theology and Culture*. Colorado Springs: NavPress, 2010.

House, H. Wayne. *Charts of Christian Theology and Doctrine*. Grand Rapids, MI: Zondervan, 1992.

Sire, James W. *Discipleship of the Mind: Learning to Love God in the Ways We Think*. Downers Grove, IL: InterVarsity, 1990.

Stone, Howard W., and James O. Duke. *How to Think Theologically*, 3rd Ed. Minneapolis: Fortress, 2013.

Unity in Diversity

Cleveland, Christena. *Disunity in Christ: Uncovering the Hidden Forces That Keep Us Apart*. Downers Grove, IL: InterVarsity, 2013.

Newbell, Trillia J. *United: Captured by God's Vision for Diversity*. Chicago: Moody, 2014.

Mentoring Resources

Here are resources that address the three pillars of the mentoring framework: *knowing and loving God, knowing your identity in Christ, and loving your neighbor*. Again, this is not an exhaustive list. It includes resources I have personally read or used for ministry.

Knowing and Loving God

Found in Him: The Joy of the Incarnation and Our Union with Christ by Elyse M. Fitzpatrick
Generous Justice: How God's Grace Makes Us Just by Timothy Keller
God as He Longs for You to See Him by Chip Ingram
The Pursuit of God by A. W. Tozer
Think Like Jesus: Make the Right Decision Every Time by George Barna

Knowing Who You Are in Christ

Brave Enough: Getting Over Our Fears, Flaws, and Failures to Live BOLD and FREE by Nicole Unice
Called: The Crisis and Promise of Following Jesus Today by Mark Labberton
Emotionally Healthy Spirituality: Unleash a Revolution in Your Life in Christ by Peter Scazzero
In the Name of Jesus: Reflections on Christian Leadership by Henri J. M. Nouwen
Lord, I Need Grace to Make It Today by Kay Arthur
Reclaiming Eve: The Identity and Calling of Women in the Kingdom of God by Suzanne Burden, Carla Sunberg, and Jamie Wright
Teach Us to Want: Longing, Ambition, and the Life of Faith by Jen Polluck Michel
The Critical Journey: Stages in the Life of Faith by Janet O. Hagberg and Robert A. Guelich
The Good and Beautiful Life: Putting on the Character of Christ by James Bryan Smith
Think Like Jesus: Make the Right Decision Every Time by George Barna
Touching the Holy: Ordinariness, Self-Esteem, and Friendship by Robert J. Wicks

What Women Tell Me: Finding Freedom from the Secrets We Keep by Anita
    Lustrea
When Life and Beliefs Collide: How Knowing God Makes a Difference by
    Carolyn Custis James

Loving Your Neighbor

A Credible Witness: Reflections on Power, Evangelism, and Race by Brenda
    Salter McNeil
Divided by Faith: Evangelical Religion and the Problem of Race in America by
    Michael O. Emerson and Christian Smith
Half the Church: Recapturing God's Global Vision for Women by Carolyn Custis
    James
Radical: Taking Back Your Faith from the American Dream by David Platt
She Did What She Could: Five Words of Jesus That Will Change Your Life by
    Elisa Morgan
The Christian Way of Living: An Ethics of the Ten Commandants by Kalus
    Bockmuehl
*The Dangerous Act of Loving Your Neighbor: Seeing Others through the Eyes of
    Jesus* by Mark Labberton
*The Just Church: Becoming a Risk-taking, Justice-seeking, Disciple-making
    Congregation* by Jim Martin
The Master Plan of Evangelism by Robert E. Coleman
The Next Evangelicalism: Freeing the Church from Western Cultural Captivity by
    Soong-Chan Rah